Facing The Truth

Bethany Storro
with
Mona Krueger

ISBN: 1-480-152-986

Dedication

To my fellow strugglers
who perceive themselves
differently from reality

May we find hope
and healing
on our journeys

Table of Contents

Foreword

I, Mona, met Bethany for the first time at the cafeteria of our local hospital. Seeing her scars made me sad because in some ways I know the road she walks.

I was burned in a car accident as an 18-year-old and lost my face to gasoline flames. The surgeries and identity reconstruction take years, a lifetime.

Bethany is only at the beginning of this process, but we feel it is important to share her journey for others who might be struggling with the same mental illness that afflicts her: Body Dysmorphic Disorder (BDD).

Many people have never heard of it. We have written this book together in hopes of raising awareness so others may seek psychological help before it takes a catastrophic toll like it did in Bethany's case. She had practically every classic symptom, undiagnosed and untreated.

Bethany has come a long way and I proudly call her a dear friend, a burn survivor and a fellow struggler. My hope is that we will hold her story gently, and with mercy.

Introduction

I, Bethany, am publishing this book not to gain attention nor sympathy, but for two reasons. One is to tell my story. The other is to bring awareness about BDD and OCD, so that others may seek help for healing.

In trying to move on with my life, I keep coming back to August 30, 2010. The need for some kind of closure compels me to try and explain what happened.

I have always been the girl down the street living a "normal life," someone seeking to find her place in this world, desiring the usual things: a good job, love, acceptance, a family. I grew up in a loving home, wanted for nothing, had close friends and plans for my life.

I now have some idea why mental illness struck me so severely, but growing up I thought I was in control, that I could handle my problems on my own. It snuck up on me.

There were signs, but being a people pleaser, not wanting to be a burden on anyone and living with a hearing impairment all contributed to my tendency to ignore them.

These are all reasons for what happened, but probably not enough for anyone's complete satisfaction in trying to understand me. I am truly sorry for the people that I hurt, misled or caused trouble for. And I wish I could prevent others from going through what I did, that they could change the course of their lives before it gets as extreme as it did in my case.

My hope in telling the truth about my journey is that someone out there might do just that, get help in the early stages of mental illness so as not to repeat the tragic events I faced. Because of the help I finally received, I feel like a different person. My life isn't easy, but it is better and I am thankful for the chance to reach out to others through these words.

Facing The Day

Chapter 1

The day was coming.

The time was right for it all to be over, one way or another. I resolved to follow through. My hatred for the monster in the mirror compelled me to act. The term *depression* seemed far too shallow to describe my sadness and hopelessness. *Deadened* or *completely and utterly uncaring* were far more accurate.

But some feelings are beyond words.

I pondered the various means (and had for several weeks), carefully doing my research for the best way to both hurt myself and ultimately die. Jumping from a bridge was too risky. I might live and end up paralyzed. That exact scenario had popped up in my online research for "stories of suicides." Cutting myself and bleeding out entered my thoughts, or perhaps taking an overdose, but having no experience with either one, I hesitated.

Lighting myself on fire seemed a possibility. With a cutter's mindset, I would punish myself by causing pain. I had never cut myself with a blade before like you hear or read about, but I had done other things. An emotional release being the goal, I needed that pain like I needed my next breath. Funny that I had wanted to feel life in me through pain.

I experimented with a lighter one morning in a chain store parking lot, not too far from my home. I had purchased one of those long butane sticks that are used for candles and such. But I couldn't go through with actually letting it touch my skin. I sat shaking and crying in my black Blazer testing it, the flame getting closer and closer. But the uncertainty stopped me. Would I burn all over? I didn't know how fire really worked and I didn't want to die right away, but rather control the focus of the pain and the damage it would cause. As a means of pain and death, fire seemed too quick and uncertain.

It's difficult to explain, but I had long thought that if my face just went away, the obsession for perfection and the horrible images I saw as a result would stop. The same could be said for my arms, my neck or the hair on my head, the body parts of choice at any given moment. My obsession would change from week to week. It had been that way for a long time. I knew the pain from hurting myself was shocking and real, lifting me from sadness and like a mass dose of adrenaline, forcing me to feel.

The guilt and the depression ate at me. It held me prisoner and I was beyond tired of it, desperate to make it all go away. This strong sense that I deserved to be punished never quite left me.

After much deliberation, I finally chose acid. It seemed a safe bet and for some not-really-logical reason, the least frightening. Most importantly, it would accomplish what the other means couldn't. It provided all the elements I desired: pain, destruction and a very good chance of death from the fumes alone, but slowly, so I could have some control.

This method I could count on. I was happy about my decision. And there was another side benefit: if it failed to kill me, at least the ugly images would be gone. My thoughts never ventured beyond that goal to the possible consequences of failure. The plan seemed sound.

I had been working the graveyard shift at a local grocery store in the bakery and deli section for several months, hiding from daytime realities with the need to sleep with the light. Shunning a social life left me with a lot of time on my hands to think and plot my demise. My excitement grew when I bought into the acid plan, to be free of the distorted, melting face that I encountered most days in the mirror. I could taste the victory over my hopelessness.

My hours of research on acid led me to a local hardware store to buy an industrial strength drain cleaner forty-eight hours before *the day*. I found it in the back corner with the plumbing products. It was packaged in a white plastic container and double bagged with a host of warning labels. I resolutely picked it up to read the instructions, glancing around a few times to make sure no one had eyes on me. The white plastic felt smooth to the touch and my hands were shaking a little as I turned to set it in my basket. It was mid-morning and the store almost empty, perfect for my plan of getting out quickly without raising suspicions.

I added a few other items on the way to the checkout counter to draw attention away from the main purchase. The clerk didn't seem fazed by the items laid out before her, though she did lecture me about the dangers of the product in the white plastic. Far from scaring me, her words gave me joy. For it not to be dangerous would waste all my hope and mental energy. This *had* to work.

I was reluctantly living with my parents at the time, the reluctance all on my side. I did it mostly for financial reasons, but also because my family had been worried about me for the past year after my divorce.

My divorce.

The regret was excruciating. I almost
wish I could say it had been messy, but a
better description would be heartbreakingly
methodical. I had walked away from someone
who loved me deeply. It fueled my need
for punishment. I knew it was too late for
reconciliation, my life such a mess. Making
anything better didn't seem remotely possible.

Back at my parents' home, I wrapped up the
acid and hid it in the back of the bathroom
vanity behind the towels and extra shampoo.
But before I went to work that night, I
snuck it back out and tested it, wanting the
reassurance that this was a viable plan.
Standing before the mirror with the acid on
the counter, I glanced at my image.

I knew myself: uncooperative dark hair, dull
brown eyes, chubby nose, freckles marring
my right cheek, premature wrinkles in various
places with a few sun spots that I hated
thrown into the mix. In the world's eyes, I was
attractive but as much as I wanted to believe
that was true, the mirror had always spoken a
different message to me.

Carefully opening the bottle with gloved
hands, I gently slipped a cotton swab into the
noxious mix and applied a tiny spot to the
right side of my cheek. It turned white and
then red, burning like crazy while dissolving a

tiny bit of tissue. The wound site was only the size of a freckle and yet the sensation of lethal pain shocked me. It continued for many long minutes. I felt exhilarated.

I was finally feeling.

The physical pain took away everything I had been enduring. At that moment my depression was gone, along with the guilt and the apathy.

But it didn't last.
Like an addict, I needed another and bigger fix.

I then resolved to pour it all over my face.

Chapter 2

The day dawned.

Monday, August 30, 2010.

I worked the usual night shift and came home about 9:00 a.m. Hoping to close my eyes for a couple of hours, I instead encountered loud construction noise both in my own house and on the street in my neighborhood. For many hearing-impaired people this would be a non-issue, but for my type of deafness it was a big deal. As an infant I had contracted spinal meningitis twice and suffered a serious hearing loss. I can only distinguish low tones and, therefore, am very much in tune with booming vibrations of machinery sounding around me, their annoyance not diminished, but maybe even magnified to my ears.

Surprisingly, my speaking ability is adequate, even remarkable for someone with my impairment, or so I have been told.

Sometimes people ask me if I am wearing a tongue ring, so I must sound slightly garbled but distinct enough to be understood. You wouldn't know I was deaf from watching me because I don't need to sign, though you might catch me reading lips and wonder.

As far as the construction noise that morning, it didn't really matter. Sleep was the least important item on my list. Getting a few last details of my life in order consumed me. I could spend hours organizing and reorganizing my world. From my earliest memories, being obsessively neat for myself and everyone around me had been an integral part of my life. If I were going to end it that day, everything had to be just so.

I snuck the acid out of the bathroom and put it in my truck, tucking it into the bottom of a bag of other supplies I had gathered for the day. For some reason the post office especially drew me. I stopped to get my mail and found a check for $920 from some bank credit. My parents had funded getting my wisdom teeth out at a cost of $900, so it felt providentially right to pay them back from this unexpected check. My mom had also bailed on the construction noise at home and was out running errands. I caught up with her at the drugstore.

She is a little shorter than I, with blondish/brown hair. For her age, my mom looks much younger and always dresses fashionably, down to the tips of her feet, usually ensconced in trendy shoes. If I had to describe her with just a few words, I would use upbeat, loving and strong. Discerning too. Not much got past her. Knowing that, I had been very careful with all that I was hiding.

She hadn't expected any payback from the wisdom teeth and was pleasantly surprised by my gift. I gave her a long hug, fighting tears and told her I loved her, thanking her for always being there for me. I left quickly before my emotions got the best of me and made her suspicious. My family knew nothing of my plans. I felt like a burden to them and wanted to lighten their load. Their knowing would crush me, and them. The load I carried was that heavy, that overwhelming.

Growing up the baby of my family, I had always been the goofy, bubbly one who loved to laugh and crack jokes, much like my dad. The Bethany I had become inside seemed disconnected from the image my loved ones had of me, and I didn't want to destroy that. Thus, I hid my real self from them, and from others.

I drove away sobbing, barely seeing the road in front of me. By then it was mid-afternoon and time to find a secluded spot to carry out my plan. The choice of a nearby park seemed perfect, mainly because I found it almost completely empty. I needed a place where no one would find me for a long while or hear my wails while the acid was taking its toll. I parked in the lot and surveyed the area, satisfied with my choice.

All my tears had left me sleepy and I caught an hour or two of rest in my Chevy. I loved that car but it also evoked bittersweet feelings. It reminded me of my ex-husband, Taylor and his deep care for me. Upon waking up, I spent some time gathering my courage by remembering why I was doing this. My thoughts ran along the lines of: *"This is what I deserve. It is the right thing to do to make it all better. I can't live with those images in the mirror any longer. I am sad for my family, but happy for me."*

As I was about ready to make an exit from the car, my cell phone vibrated. It was my sister, Willow, texting me. My sister had always been my sounding board and encourager, helping to draw me back from the edge of whatever rebellious brink I was on. Her words, as usual, went straight to the heart of things:

> *"For some reason I just feel like I need to text you and tell you that you don't have to punish yourself. We love you. God loves you. Just the way you are."*

Those words gave me pause.

But I didn't let them stop me. Setting the phone gently back on the seat by my purse, I left the vehicle with my bag of destruction.

The day was mild for August, lightly cloudy and hinting at rain. I breathed in the smell of fresh cut grass as I determinedly walked toward a cement structure in the middle of the park next to the playground. It contained several individual bathrooms. I slipped inside one of them and firmly closed the door behind me, blowing out a breath of relief that no one had stopped me or questioned me. For some reason the lock wouldn't catch but I didn't concern myself about it.

The small room contained a toilet to the left and a sink on the far right without windows or a mirror. It had one small light fixture on the ceiling, leaving the place with a dark and dingy feel. The temperature inside was cool, and it seemed poorly ventilated, perfect for what I wanted.

It had a dank, metallic smell mixed with the usual toilet odors wafting up from the bowl, but it was quiet and I felt like the only person left in the universe. As I thought about moving forward, my hands started to shake and my stomach started rolling. I ignored them both.

I crouched down in the corner and inventoried my supplies on the floor in front of me: acid, gloves, cotton swabs, towels and small mirror. Donning the gloves to protect my hands, I resolutely opened the bottle. Getting high would give me courage and help with the pain somewhat, so I stayed in that position for a

11

while, maybe twenty minutes, just breathing in the fumes with my hands cupped around the small opening.

It made me dizzy. My whole body increasingly shook and my breathing became labored. My head began to throb as I felt my lungs tightening. The final step of the plan was to drink the acid so I had to ignore these things and keep going.

Endure.

Fortunately, the craving for pain hadn't diminished and I was counting on it working for me.

I reached for the first cotton swab and stuck it in the bottle, dripping a little on my glove while pulling it back out. The sight of the drops eating through what was supposed to be acid-retardant material horrified me and thrilled me at the same time. Another drop spilled on the cement floor, began to sizzle and turn a brownish copper color, eating through the cement.

My thoughts kept churning out a couple of lines, like a mantra: *"Finally. I won't have a face. All of my problems – disappearing, disappearing..."*

I applied a test run to my right cheek along a line from my ear to my mouth, having to hurry because the cotton swab was dissolving fast.

My heart stopped. The pain was indescribable.

I jumped to my feet and ran to the sink, gasping out loud muffled screams. I grabbed the bar by the sink with one hand, standing there with my whole body clenched, trying to endure and let the acid do its damage. A few drops had dripped on my shirt, small holes burning through to my bra. It became quickly clear that cotton swabs were not efficient enough. My endurance was weakening and my right glove was melting. I knew I had to make this go faster.

First I poured some drain cleaner directly on my left cheek with the liquid splattering here and there. Then I decided to douse a towel and hold it to my face. My hated nose got special attention. I went into a frenzy, screaming and crying, barely staying conscious while resolutely holding the towel tightly to my skin. I wondered why I wasn't passing out from the fumes, let alone the pain.

One hundred knives jabbing me.
My body and mind in shock from the agony.

I shed the right glove because parts of it had melted into shreds. But giving up wasn't part of my game plan, so I kept maneuvering a way to keep the acid on my face. I tried to grit my teeth against the pain but it was becoming less and less endurable. I peeled

13

the towel away and tossed it on the floor.
Frantically grabbing the little mirror to check
my progress, I saw a huge and swollen face in
the small circle, the acid bubbling and sizzling.
The sight made me cry out.

The driven part of me fought to not give up. It
felt so good and so horribly bad at the same
time. It hit me that I didn't seem to be dying,
but the thought of drinking the acid, that final
step, was unbearable. I couldn't take any
more pain. It was like being on fire.

I turned to the sink to splash water on
my face, hoping to dilute the excruciating
sensations so I could try again in a little bit.
The tap sputtered air. I had a water bottle with
me and splattered what was left of it on me,
but the chemicals were too strong for it to
make a difference. *"What have I done, what
have I done, what have I done?"* I chanted.
My thoughts were jumbled and confused.

I needed help.
Me, who never asked for help.
Or felt like I deserved it.
I began crying out to God in my head.

Grabbing what remained of the drain cleaner
and leaving the rest behind, I ran into the
park desperately looking around, and saw
no one. My Blazer was near. I hopped in and
threw the acid on the passenger seat, driving
several blocks to try and find an area with lots
of people. I remember thinking I had to hide

my actions somehow because they were so dark and shameful. After throwing the acid into a bin from my car window, I kept driving and searching for someone to help me.

I ended up downtown in a business district and remembered there was a coffee shop right around the corner. I kept driving farther along the street and pulled over haphazardly to stop. I flung myself out of the vehicle, dropping my keys and leaving the door wide open.

The pain had me in a frenzy. I ran down the sidewalk crying for help, at one point dropping to the ground with my face in my hands. A man approached and asked me if I was okay. I saw in a blur more people beginning to gather with concern around me. It was hard to read lips with my body convulsing and on the verge of blacking out. I remember one question, *"Are you okay?"* Another mouthing, *"Stay with us, stay with us."*

One of the bystanders called 911 and it took some minutes for an ambulance to come. Life was getting blurrier and blurrier around me. I wished I were dying just to escape the unrelenting pain from the acid still eating through my skin.

I vaguely remember one person forming the words, *"Did someone hurt you?"* Making up a story of someone else's involvement was never part of the plan, but being in no condition to explain my actions at the moment, I simply blurted out, *"Yes – Help – Yes!"*

And then the world went blank.

Chapter 3

The nightmare began.
I woke up.

It all came flooding back to me lying there in
the ER later that evening. My face felt swollen
and the small exam room chilly. The shaking
began deep inside. My parents stood around
my bed telling me how sorry they were that
someone had hurt me like this. I opened
my mouth to come clean about what really
happened and then froze.

I wasn't ready.
And the coward in me cringed at the truth.

Looking into my father's eyes, I couldn't risk
the disappointment reality would foster. How
could I explain the monster in the mirror?
Hurting myself? Desiring death? My parents
were such good people. The truth would
destroy them. It had to stay hidden. My
shame stemmed from a deep place no one

knew about and telling my family the truth seemed worse than being eaten by acid, or getting in trouble with the police, or having the world hate me.

An hour later I was told the media wanted to meet with me. I pondered that for a moment, but fear kept me from saying no. What excuse could I give? Everyone now believed someone had hurt me and they needed information from me to find this person. In my panic, lying to cover my behavior seemed my only option. A small press conference couldn't be such a big deal, right? Still in a state of shock and completely naive, I thought if I gave the police this one lie then it would all be over, that the story would die fast.

Tomorrow. I would come clean then. I just needed a little more time to muster up some courage.

Unbeknownst to me, the media circus had already started bellowing loud shouts to far corners of the country, and my lies to protect myself would take on monumental consequences I was heedlessly unaware of.

I got an inkling of it when the detective walked into my room. This was after my surgeon had taken me into the operating room to do some basic debridement of my scabbed and wounded face. The damage from the chemical was extensive, especially to my chin, left cheek and nose, where I had held the acid-soaked towel for so long.

Feeling rather out of it from the pain medication, I nevertheless knew this man held the key to my story being believed. I didn't plot to think up wild details to add, but instead just went along with the flow. Agreeing with everything and saying as little as possible would protect that lie for one more day, just one more day.

The detective was somewhat tall, stocky, with brown-turning-gray hair and watchful eyes. I felt intimidated by the sight of him walking into my room. His questions started out simple. *"Can you describe the woman who did this?"* *"It's all kind of muddled in my head..."* I vaguely replied.

Snowballing.

Like an avalanche my words kept sweeping down some horrible boulder-filled path and gaining more and more momentum to devastate my future. *"What did she look like? Did she have white skin?"* *"No, kind of dark,"* I reported. With a small African American community in my city, I figured the police would have a really hard time finding anyone like the person I described. I grabbed for details in some far recess of my imagination, my attitude defensive because I knew none of it was true.

The police wondered how my eyes could have

been protected in the attack. I told them I had purchased sunglasses right before the incident at a local store, not thinking that this lie was easily found out by checking surveillance cameras.

Nothing mattered then. I was feeling so hopeless, confused and dead inside. The plan to hurt myself had gone so horribly wrong. The new plan unfolding, which wasn't a plan at all, had its own momentum that carried me along in its path. I would say anything to get it over with quickly and end the inquiry. He took down my words and commented little. It was hard to look him in the eye. My guilt and shame weighed my head down.

I wanted a place to hide from everything and everyone, but reality intruded.

I was transferred over to the burn center, a closed unit that offered me more protection from the outside world. The next morning I made the mistake of opening up the blinds and saw a crowd of reporters outside my window. The extent of attention focused on me began to sink in a little. This seemed beyond local. What had I done? How far had the news traveled?

My doctor at the burn center decided not to graft the wounds on my face right away, wanting to see how they would heal on their own. They changed the bandages every other day and kept close watch on my progress, but a long hospital stay was not necessary at this point.

My room had quickly filled up with balloons, food baskets, cards, pretty fake flower arrangements and stuffed animals to cheer me. The cards were signed by the staff of Oprah, Dr. Phil and a host of other media outlets who wanted to stay on top of the story.

What had this become? It all felt surreal.

People from across the world sent me messages, expressing their care and wishes for my healing. Little kids and local families gave gifts to encourage me, and these sweet offerings made me feel the most guilty.

A parade of people stopped by wanting to see me every day, an outpouring of love and concern I was unprepared for and didn't deserve, nor want.

If it weren't for the panic gurgling inside me, waiting for the ax to fall, I would have enjoyed the attention. I dreaded having to keep lying, trying to maintain a cohesive and consistent story when it was all fiction. Reading through the text messages and Facebook comments, there were moments when I wished someone else *had* done this to me and I could actually receive the kind words of others. All the concern just heaped more torment on my scared conscience.

The day my ex-husband, Taylor, came to visit marks the closest I got to blurting out the truth to someone. I wanted to tell him so badly but I lacked courage and let the opportunity pass.

In a week's time, I left the burn center and went back to my parents' house. I had to apply a special salve twice a day to keep the wounds on my face moist and to kill bacteria that could result in an infection. Sections of it were scabbed over and I looked frightful, but those truly horrible images I often saw in the mirror were leaving me alone at the moment. The acid-damaged skin staring back at me was minor in comparison.

Donations started coming in from so many Good Samaritans captured by my story. Cameras hovered outside the windows of my parents' home and stacks of cards piled up in my mailbox. People raised funds and opened bank accounts on my behalf; texts and emails poured in with sympathy. Why did people have to care so much? Why couldn't this all just go away? They saw me as a victim, but I was the perpetrator.

I was not enjoying the focus on me, and the reality of looming consequences plagued my waking hours. Spending a lot of time holed up in my bedroom and in a constant state of stress, my mind reeled with self-recrimination and hatred. I sat on my bed at night awake for hours, trying to figure out what to do to get out of the mess I had gotten myself into.

I began to prepare myself mentally for the arrest. And for the world's hatred.

The cops were coming soon.
I deserved punishment.
An even greater one.

What would jail be like? How long would I be there? Years? How would I be treated? Would I be bullied or beaten? Was I strong enough to endure? The thought of prison had never existed in my reality before. Not hearing might spare me the taunts of other women prisoners. Could I call that a bright spot in my dark ponderings?

Surprisingly, plans to take my life to escape it all weren't plaguing me at this moment, but instead I consoled myself with the thought that I could rebuild my life when the chaos was over.

Start fresh somewhere.
Maybe.

My parents encouraged me to spend some of the money pouring in and knowing a refusal would raise questions, I went along with them. I used funds from my regular bank account, which included only a small portion of the gifts that had come in mixed with my personal money. Two other accounts had been set up by Good Samaritans that I never had access to, nor wanted to.

I didn't buy a ton of things like the media portrayed. I picked up a pair of pants, pajamas and hygiene products, items I would have purchased on a normal basis. Not really keeping track of the exact amount of my own money, I also picked up the tab for some food for my family from a local restaurant. Spending money when I was hurting had been a bad habit for me growing up. Knowing my current predicament, I should have been more careful.

Some of my dad's colleagues at work collected a sum of money as a gift. Because I didn't have a computer, my family thought I should buy a tablet. After the purchase, I pretended to be unhappy with it, secretly planning to return it to the store as soon as I could and setting up the excuse in advance.

I felt like a rat in a cage with so much interest focused on me. My mom, sensing I needed to get away from the craziness, took the train with me up to Seattle to visit my sister, Willow. A kindred spirit, Willow had always been the dearest person in the world to me. But I was hiding so much, even from her. I knew I had to tell the truth soon, just not the how of it. Various scenarios kept playing in my head. Do I just blurt it out? One clean rip like the scabs they scraped off my injured face? Nothing could make this less painful for the people I loved.

Opting out of an excursion to the mall in order to be alone, I spent some time hashing it out in my head. My sister lived in a beautiful part of the country with a view of Puget Sound from her balcony, but sadness and exhaustion found me in a darkened room oblivious to it all. I tried to sleep but those restless thoughts kept me awake.

The idea of suicide slipped in again. Part of me wanted the coward's way out, to let my family find out the truth after I was gone. Or maybe I could just run away in order to avoid the consequences staring so clearly at me. Both options brought tears of hopelessness mixed with remorse.

A verse from the New Testament, *"the truth shall set you free,"* rumbled over and over in my head, tormenting me but also offering an elusive bit of hope. My prayers to God became desperate. I pleaded for a way to circumvent the nightmare.

But His gentle whispers to me made it clear that my only course was to tell the truth.

And soon.

Chapter 4

How had I gotten here?

I found myself asking this question on a fairly regular basis. My childhood had been ideal, or as close to ideal as one can get for someone who couldn't hear very well. I grew up surrounded by people who cherished me.

The year of my birth was 1982, and the meningitis hit extremely early, the first occurrence as a two-week old. My mom called the doctor after noticing that I had a fever. I guess babies that little don't normally get them. They rushed me to the hospital and I spent weeks there fighting for my life from the viral form of the disease. Eight months later I contracted bacterial meningitis, which carried the same level of severity.

I almost died both times.

My small community in Northern Idaho

rallied and members of my church rushed to the hospital to pray with my parents, who were frantic for my life and grateful for the support. I believe God answered their prayers and spared me. Because I could hear low-pitched sounds and seemed to be responding normally at home, my hearing loss didn't become apparent until I was around two years old. A volunteer at the nursery in church first wondered about my hearing when I didn't react to her voice.

After doing a round of tests, the doctors discovered that while my lower tones came out close to normal, the higher tones were almost non-existent. This meant I could hear a semi truck booming by but not the high pitch of a fire alarm that most people would be covering their ears for the pain of it. The audiologists gave me the technical diagnosis of *profound deafness*.

I am the youngest of three. My sister Willow is six years older and my brother Abraham, or Abe, as we call him, is three years older. Willow, the studious one, seemed the typical first born, bent on care-taking and being responsible to play her proper role in my growing up years. Abe, an easy-going kind of guy, was the protective big brother, someone I could always count on to watch out for me. No one took my existence for granted and my siblings especially doted on me.

My parents grew up in the Chicago area, met

each other at a swing dance competition, won it and then fell in love. They decided they wanted to live in the Northwest and started out in Alaska, followed by a move to Idaho. My dad has always been the happiest when working outdoors with his hands, building or repairing something. His loyalty and honesty have long been traits that draw people to him. He worked full days at a paper mill, while my mom taught math classes at our school.

They recall how much trouble I got into as a smiling, fun-loving toddler. With a hearing loss, my heightened sense of sight and touch fed my explorer tendencies. One day I got into a package of dye. Delighted by its color and texture, I drew happy pictures on the bathroom walls and my clothing. Soon after I discovered oil paints and this time the living room rug was my canvas. My mom discovered my artwork and instead of getting mad, just had to laugh, though she did call poison control for a remedy in case I had ingested anything.

I loved peanut butter and honey, but more to create with than to eat. They ended up all over me and on counter tops and floors. My mom would often walk into the kitchen and see my chubby little thighs sticking out of a cupboard, dripping in honey or some other food product. The tactile exploration helped me to learn what my mostly silent world missed in sounds.

At church my parents would lead worship and had to leave me in the pews for sections of time. I had a habit of exploring ladies' bags, seeking out any kind of makeup to play with, especially lip stick. Red-faced, my mom would apologize for my behavior as I impishly perused for the next purse in my line of vision, but the ladies caught on to me and would joke about it, holding tight to their handbags if I came anywhere near.

No one ever taught me to read lips. It just came naturally as I learned to interpret the happenings around me, though it took many years to hone my skill. Speech classes from toddlerhood on helped me to form sounds properly. My pronunciation never became perfect, or so I have been told, but I can communicate well.

A few of my hard-to-articulate words from childhood became a part of our family lexicon. We all say *chop-chop* for ketchup and *mustrub* for mustard. My family had fun with it and even the neighbors got into the silliness when I asked for things on my hot dog that they had to decipher.

Lip readers can't distinguish the "ch" sound from the "sh". This one provided a few funny mishaps over the years. My version of the movie title *Chitty Chitty Bang Bang*, sung off-key in the school hallway, definitely got a few smiles and snickers as I went on my merry way.

It is interesting what stands out as I think about my childhood. I was ten years old before being introduced to the wonderful world of closed caption TV. It changed my relationship with the big black box. Before closed caption I never liked it. The Muppets bored me because they didn't really have lips to read. Other segments on Sesame Street weren't any better with kids running around aimlessly. Tom and Jerry claimed the prize as my favorite cartoon because there was no spoken dialogue involved and the activity actually had purpose that I could understand.

While other kids would ooh and aah over Cinderella and Bambi, my thoughts ran along the lines of, *"Who is the lady with the sparkling wand?"* and *"What is Bambi really up to?"* With closed caption television, I revisited them and finally understood the nuances of the plots without having to ask my sister or mom a ton of questions.

Willow and I had a room together. It was very pink. We had bunk beds and like the fate of all little sisters, I got stuck with the lower bunk. I shared it with about fifty soft creatures including Cabbage Patch dolls, cute fuzzy puppies and stuffed bears. I had a ritual that every night I would place them on the floor one by one, with their eyes facing down because it scared me if they were lying there staring up at me. In the morning I would carefully place them all back on my bed in perfect order, eyes facing out.

Willow and I couldn't talk at night in the dark like other sisters do, so we would play a silly game instead to connect with one another. She would lean down from the top bunk and I would reach up and touch parts of her face, *guessing* what my fingers came into contact with and giggling when I got them wrong.

During the day we would play office with our collection of used paper, staplers, tape and a lovely old business-size book of checks. Writing checks became my specialty. Being a lover of organization, my secretarial skills were unmatched by any other six-year-old in the city limits. Willow declared herself the boss and kept me busy, though even in our dorky, pretend world I was still deaf so she had to answer all phone calls. We changed our names. Willow became Rene and I was Deanne. We declared ourselves total nerds and enjoyed the world only she and I lived in.

Just because we could.

That's not to make it sound like we never fought, because we did. Usually we squabbled over clothes after attempting to sneak things out of each other's closets.

Abe and I fought less. With him I would pretend to be a waitress, taking his order on my small notepad by checking off the grilled cheese box or the one that said BLT.

Proceeding to the kitchen, I would hang up his order on the hanging light fixture, make the sandwich and yell, "New order up!"

Like any younger sister, I demanded my fair share of attention. And being gregarious, I gathered friends around me from whatever sphere I could find them.

My best friend, the pastor's daughter, lived next door to me. Our backyard fence had a gate, affording direct access to each other. Naphtali and I loved playing together, dressing up, planning our weddings, laughing and sharing those little girl thoughts that shaped our dreams.

Playing with Barbie dolls was probably our favorite pastime. We had all of the paraphernalia: the house, beds, tables, chairs, fake food, clothes and accessories galore. It took us hours to set up and just when we were ready to actually start playing, we would look at each other and say, *Do you wanna do something else?"* It became a standing joke between us.

Naphtali and I also had a passion for the days of old when women dressed in frilly long gowns, coiffed their hair in buns and carried parasols. We would wander the neighborhood in our getup and usually end up at the local candy store called the Sugarplum. The old-fashioned kind of candy drew us as well: candy sticks, licorice and gumdrops.

I never hesitated to part with my allowance for a splurge on candy but I had to convince my friend to part with any of her coins. I thought she was far too frugal for someone who was only eight years old. I had to cajole her to live a little. Fifty cents seemed to be her tolerated limit while I had no such inhibition.

Even with our differences, our most sincere dream was to find the love of our lives and to be as close as a fence away. Keeping loved ones near always concerned me.

We had two beloved dachshunds as pets, Cosmo and Judie. Their ears became mine as they alerted me to people at our front door and other noises that I couldn't hear. One time I had put some chicken in the oven and had forgotten about it. The fire alarm went off and I didn't hear a peep or smell any smoke. Cosmo, on the other hand, went ballistic, running back and forth between the kitchen and where I sat in the living room.

I saw the panic in his sweet eyes and followed him to the source. He saved the day. After that, whenever he saw me in the kitchen he would dart out, fearing I would burn something again. I loved having him near, both for companionship and protection.

Two very cherished people in my life were my grandparents. They lived nearby on the Pend Oreille River in Idaho and owned a quaint and comfortable house filled with old-fashioned furniture. Delicious smells constantly emanated from my grandma's kitchen. A favorite tradition with my grandpa involved sitting on his lap and leaning back to watch his lips while he read the cartoons from the paper. My love of board games came from him. Board games were visual and didn't require a lot of communication so they especially drew me.

Any time I could spend with my loved ones meant a lot to me. My family was close and we would take trips to the Pacific Coast for vacations. I loved the flashing lights of the arcade and pitting my skills against the mechanical machines to win a coveted soft toy to sit on my bed. I loved the feel of seashells and the sand between my toes, the cold breeze on my cheeks. I experienced so many fun and normal childhood things that never gave me cause to think I lacked or was in anyway inferior to those around me.

I cherished each and every memory.

And it made me wonder how such an innocent childhood could have ended in such trauma.

Chapter 5

What had I learned?

I loved school and attended a private Christian academy associated with my church, where the classrooms were small and everyone knew each other. The school went a long way toward mitigating the effects of my disability, although no school could have completely done that.

My graduating class had only eight students and certain subjects were combined with other grades. With my hearing loss, I did best one-on-one, so always being in a group at school made communication an interesting challenge, but one I tackled head-on.

In the classroom, I had to focus my attention and gather as much information as I could. My teachers really tried to remember not to turn their backs when speaking, and at times had to become contortionists, writing on the chalkboard and yet allowing me to read their lips. When my fellow students would ask questions, my eyes had to search quickly to pinpoint the source in order to catch on to the back-and-forth dialogue.

We experimented with hearing aids and I wore two big beige ones that wrapped completely around my ears for a while. They helped somewhat but could also become annoying, making the sounds louder but not necessarily clearer. I took them off sometimes out of pure frustration.

One day I forgot to turn off the little switch on one of them and blissfully unaware, slipped the device into the storage space under the top of my desk. It was emitting a high-pitched piercing tone that bounced off the walls of our little classroom. My teacher searched and searched for this mysterious noise, while I sat inches away from it, observing the scurrying of bodies around the room. The pastor even came in and began to look up into the ceiling panels for the source.

We tore the room apart until a student got close to my desk and figured out I was the cause of the uproar. Any disruption of class was considered a good thing, so my classmates liked me even more as we laughed about the incident. Smiling, they just shook their heads saying, "Oh, Bethany."

My fellow students teased me once in a while

for my *interesting* pronunciation of words, but they weren't mean about it. I felt accepted and a part of the group. Once in a while it seemed excessive and my feelings did get hurt, but I would laugh along with them in order to hide it.

As far as grades, I was a better-than-average student but never got straight A's. My mom taught mathematics at my school during the day and then continued to work with me when she got home. Every evening she would help me study to catch up on anything I had missed and prepare for tests to stay on track. Algebra and geometry were my nemeses, but I liked English and history. With my mom's help, I could write a mean essay and the other students liked my stories, probably because they were fanciful and full of humor.

In junior high I decided to join band class and play the clarinet. Music made me come alive because I could feel the beat of the drums and that throbbing sunk into the creative part of me. I could hear myself play the low tones of my chosen instrument and stay in tune, but the upper range was another story.

The tricky thing for any new clarinet player is to control the squeaking. My first concert brought me great pleasure, but I found out later that the audience didn't quite feel the same way. While I was in my own little happy world squawking away and oblivious to it, some in the crowd were fighting to not cover their ears.

Needless to say, my career as a clarinet prodigy didn't last long.

But with the dance team, I found a niche. It was organized, precise and fit me perfectly. Because I felt the beat from my toes on up and had some natural ability, I could move well. Eventually I even became the leader of the team.

During my school years, dancing gave me the greatest joy. I liked the idea of break dancing, but could never find a good teacher. Ballet seemed too girly. I compromised on hip hop and as early as ten years old, started taking classes to improve my skill. My friend, Laura, and I became partners and performed exceptionally well together, an impressive duet that rivaled the best of dancers around us. We committed ourselves totally to our chosen sport.

Dancing put me in touch with the music and swept me away from the norm. And for those moments I felt special, exhilarated, on top of the world.

Adaptability.

I learned to manage my life, to get involved and find ways to cope. Not wanting to be a burden on anyone, I kept hurts and concerns private. But so did a lot of my classmates.

Like everyone else, trial and error were
my teachers. I thrived in some areas and
floundered in others. I tried to make use of
my strengths and minimize my weak areas.

Just like everyone else.
Or so I thought.

But I am getting ahead of myself.
Back to facing the truth.

Chapter 6

The cops beat me to it.

On the train ride back from Seattle, my mind was racing with thoughts of the best plan possible to confess that very day. But by the time my mom and I pulled up to the curb of our home, the police had already surrounded the place. My dad had answered the door when they came pounding on it and asked for my computer, camera, journals - a stack of stuff to use for evidence.

I saw my dad sitting out on the porch with his head in his hands. The dread took hold of me. I tried to breathe deeply, willing down the panic, my heart pounding, waiting for him to approach us. My mom was looking around at the commotion mystified.

The look in his eyes.
Unforgettable.
Seared into my heart forever.

My darkest day.

I had been dreading this for a reason.

My dad asked me a simple question, *"Did you do this to yourself?"* I didn't answer right away, not wanting to face the truth, nor hurt him. He asked me again, *"Bethany, did you do this?"* I finally blurted out, *"Yes"* and gutted him with my answer. I didn't catch the tone of his voice but my observant eyes saw the pain and betrayal clearly written on his face. And then came the scalding tears. He threw the search warrant in the car and exclaimed that nothing would ever be the same again.

He had been suspicious of my answers for several days prior, when I could never quite look him in the eye while fumbling to respond to his pointed questions. But being my loyal father, he had doggedly stuck by me as his daughter, choosing to believe me when many signs started pointing to the facts not adding up.

I felt numb, out of body, sick to my stomach. That feeling stayed with me as the police took me away to the station, leaving my stunned parents behind, reeling from the truth.

I was led into a conference room and interviewed. It didn't have one of those double mirrors, just sterile concrete walls, a table and a few metal chairs. For the first time I let some of the details come out, though my answers were a bit jumbled as I didn't always understand the gist of the questions mouthed at me or the assumptions behind them. A panicked mental state can preclude coherency.

I hadn't preplanned to blame someone else for my acid burns, only to somehow hide the shame of what I had done. The detectives had all assumed I had lied for money or for attention, apparently having known of my guilt since the second day after the incident. The suicide motive was an unexpected twist to the story.

When they left me alone briefly in the room, I searched for a sharp object. Seeing nothing useful, I ended up using my jacket to try and suffocate myself. Any reason to live had been wiped out. I felt I had no foreseeable future. Coming back into the room, the detective interrupted my attempted self-destruction, but the reprieve was temporary. I vowed to keep searching for a means.

They then ushered me into my parents' conference room right next door. I could tell my mom had been crying and I knew they had a million questions. We sat there for a moment, heads down, barely looking at each other, pain and lingering shock between us. My mom, red-eyed and pleading, asked the first with a sob: *"Why didn't you say something? You know you can come to us."*

I was numb, speechless. I had never seen her

cry so hard. Normally my mom is the most upbeat person in my world and her pain tore at me.

My dad, still upset and overwhelmed with disbelief, voiced his disappointment and disillusionment with my behavior. What could I say? I had no defense or excuses. Being sorry covered very little ground at the moment. He eventually calmed down and agreed with my mom that I needed psychological help. I hadn't done this to destroy their lives. But they, unfortunately, became collateral damage in my actions. Mercifully, they stood by me and promised not to abandon me. I desperately clung to their love and loyalty.

The detective informed us that I wasn't under arrest.

Yet.

It would take some time to sift through the evidence and charges. When I begged to go home with my parents, the detectives asked me outright if I would try and hurt myself again. I couldn't deny the possibility. Sending me to a nearby hospital for psychological evaluation seemed a wise plan that my parents agreed with.

I was on suicide watch.

The basement psych area was my final destination for the day, but first an assessment was made in the main hospital building. My parents discreetly drove me over there from the police station. The lobby had several televisions for visitors to watch. Walking in the door, I saw pictures of myself plastered all over with the headlines, *"Breaking News"* and *"Hoax."* I saw angry faces call me names and mouth, *"How dare she!"* My dad made me turn my face away to block it out.

But the sickness in my stomach churned harder.

Sitting in a room dressed in a little blue safe-suit, even my hair ties taken from me, reality began to hit. My pastor came to see me at the hospital and looking at him made me sob. For the first time I wondered if my behavior was normal. *"Who would do something like this?"* I asked. *"But look at me,"* I tried to reason, *"This face shouldn't be here."* I wanted to convince him of my logic, but he shook his head sadly and conveyed reality to me. *"Bethany, it's okay. No. Generally people do not try to hurt themselves like this. But you're going to get help."*

He didn't change my mindset but I pondered his words for days, being stuck in lockdown, evaluated, given different meds and watched carefully. Having always taken my freedom for granted, it felt wrong to be held somewhere against my will.

Depressed, completely frightened and restless, I kept trying to think of a way to take my life to end the nightmare.

In the meantime my parents were scrambling to deal with the media lined up and down our block and beyond. That first night after the hoax unveiling, they didn't even attempt to return home, but stayed with friends instead. Within a couple days they decided to give a press conference to dampen down the deluge.

Another huge task for them was to find legal counsel for me. One of our neighbors came to the rescue, even though this type of case didn't fit his specialty as a lawyer. My case would require long hours of hard work and we did not have a lot of money.

Knowing that some other firm could use my pain for publicity compelled my neighbor and his partner to take on the job. They began to meet with me to prepare me for my first court date. I was being charged with theft for the donations I took under false pretenses, and for giving false statements to the police.

I had been forced to tell the truth and part of me thanked God for hearing my desperate cries for help. Though my darkest day still seemed overwhelming and the consequences shadowed my waking hours, a small sense of relief seeped into my conscious thoughts. Finally it was out and not buried in me with its crushing weight.

The truth.

But I didn't know if I could trust my concept of it. My world felt so scrambled. I knew what I had done but not the why of it all.

As I faced an unforeseeable future, I felt a long way from true freedom.

Chapter 7

I counted the days.

It had been two weeks from my failed suicide attempt until the *hoax* became unveiled, and another two weeks on suicide watch before my first court appearance. Each day in lockdown felt like a month and I hated being there, the cold impersonal room, cut off from everyone.

My mom brought me my phone one day and I viewed hundreds of text messages from my friends and acquaintances. Some outright rejected me, while others were confused and upset. None of them touched the cold place in my heart that felt dead and hopeless.

None of them knew my desperation.

I had to shut down my Facebook page because of the media onslaught. A few last comments struck painfully deep. My beloved ex, Taylor, posted that he was sick to his stomach after hearing the news report. The person in my life who knew me the most intimately never thought I could have done something like this. What did that say about me? Maybe I *was* that monster in the mirror all the way through to my core.

Sleep eluded me for several days prior to the court date. I felt overwhelmed and panicky. Lockdown was awful, but it had also become my new norm and a place of temporary safety. The staff didn't treat me like a monster. They understood mental illness and didn't come across judgmental or callous.

My lawyers told me to wear simple clothing, which turned into black slacks and a blue button-down shirt. I was still at the beginning stages of physical healing, the skin on my face tender and rash-like. My nose required a thick gauze pad because it was open and oozing.

It was time to face a world that now hated me.

Expecting a fair amount of media attention, we made a plan to arrive at the courthouse and get in the building as quickly as possible. My dad dropped my mom and me off near the back entrance, and my lawyers met us there. We were whisked inside fairly unnoticed because most of the press were camped out front.

We reviewed our statements in a side room

until the bailiff called us in before the judge. My lawyers warned me of the crowd in the courtroom, but I wasn't prepared for the huge camera pointed at me when I walked in. Or the flashing lights. I tried to calm my racing heart, telling myself that it would be over soon. Appearing before the judge was quick. I pleaded not guilty to the charges of theft. My lawyers asked for an extension to put together a more thorough defense.

In the meantime, I agreed to seek professional help for an extended period of time. My parents had found a treatment center with a one-year program for psychological evaluation and counseling. The plan was for me to check into this facility after my court appearance. I signed the paperwork and followed my team out of the room.

Leaving the courthouse was much more difficult than arriving, as reporters swarmed near and began shouting at me. I felt the vibration of their booming tones. I saw someone's lips saying, *"Why did you do this?"* They bombarded me with questions and made my heart pound with their demanding energy.

The mass of reporters and cameras followed us to our vehicle. We raced away from the courthouse, seeing a few cars following, but eventually we lost them. We killed time by driving around for a while and then snuck over to the mental health facility to drop off my things. I had an appointment with my burn surgeon and it bought us some more time to avoid the places where anyone would expect us.

The mental health facility was our final stop of the day and by the time we arrived, the besieging media had given up and gone home, waiting for another day. The facility ended up hiring a guard to keep them at bay. The phone calls to my family and knocks on our front door, however, didn't stop for weeks. It was hard for any of us to imagine life ever being normal again. Still reeling from the events of the day, I tearfully said goodbye to my mom and barricaded myself in my room.

About 35 people lived in this facility at any given time. I knew no one and it was the last place on earth I wanted to be, especially for an entire year: 365 days to slowly and painfully count down.

Four walls, a single bed with a lumpy mattress, dresser and small sink described my new living quarters. The first night I threw a blanket on the bed and slept in my clothes, not venturing from that spot until the middle of the next day. One of the staff knocking on my door finally aroused me.

I stayed cocooned for four days, not eating, mostly trying to lose myself in sleep, only sneaking out a few times to use the bathroom.

I just hadn't counted on living.

Nor what the consequences of my actions would be.

Did I even comprehend yet how much help I needed? Who could I count on at this new place? Would anyone understand me? I felt so lost and alone.

God seemed distant and I tried to blame my misery on Him. Didn't He care? Or know the future? I struggled with the He-let-this-happen kinds of thoughts. Why was I still alive? Upset at everything and everyone, getting out of bed seemed pointless.

A journal entry from those first few days conveys my frame of mind:

> *"Is this really happening? How has my life turned to this? I am sure I have lost all my friends growing up, new friends I made. After admitting that I made the story up because I was afraid to let people know that I wanted to end my life and did not want to live with those negative thoughts, I am sure my family will not be able to take anymore, and leave. I have never felt so alone.*
>
> *The picture right now is this: tiny room, blank white walls, a small window that looks out to more rooms with windows, people walking the halls that I do not know. So small and so cold here.*

How lonely and ashamed I feel in this moment. I cannot think besides my divorce of a time I have cried so much. I can barely see what I am writing.

Why, God? What have I done? How can I go on with my life with the whole world knowing now, that I am someone who wanted to destroy her own face and to attempt suicide? I do not know how I am going to get through this. I think of ways in this very moment of attempting to just end it again. Are there any sharp objects? No strings? What can I use?

No point in going on.

I need to get some sleep. It is 3:00 a.m. Maybe later on today will be better. Anything has to be better than what I am feeling right now."

The next morning my own stench finally got me out of my room for more than two minutes as I headed for a long shower. Vanity can be a good thing sometimes, and hunger had set in. My counselor stood in line with me for the first food run at the cafeteria. We found a table together. The other residents seemed to be staring a hole in my back and they unnerved me.

Frantic calls to my mom and my sister left me with some advice: take it one day at a time.

They told me that even though I found myself in a terrible storm, it wouldn't last forever, that God would never leave me without hope or a way through.

I had nothing else to count on.

Chapter 8

The mirror spoke to me.

My little room sported none except for a tiny makeup mirror I used to put on mascara. I wouldn't let the mirror drop farther down than the level of my eyes. It was better not to look at what I had done to myself.

The bathroom mirror posed a bigger challenge. A staff person would wait for me outside the door to make sure I didn't linger. It wasn't the current image that would terrify me, but older, more horrific ones.

And I never knew when they would pop up.

If you have ever been to a haunted house, you have experienced those mirrors that distort the body in a grotesque way. Those are the kinds of images I would see when I gazed at my reflection.

If I stared at myself for any length of time, one side of my face would elongate, leaving my eye bulging out. The skin would snap back in place, only to distort the other half in similar fashion. I would close my eyes trying, to no avail, to lose the image, becoming almost mesmerized by the monster-like creature facing me.

This had happened to me for a long time.

The first counselor I met with had labeled my problem the first time she saw me on the news: Body Dysmorphic Disorder (BDD). It is a chronic mental illness in which you cannot stop thinking about a flaw in your appearance, a flaw that is either minor or imagined. Long hours staring at mirrors can bring on illusions that terrify. Add in untreated and extreme obsessive compulsive tendencies mixed with depression, and you have the cocktail that brought me to this place.

If only I had known that my problem had a name.

If only.

The counselor guessed a lot of my obsessive history before I ever opened my mouth and I was astounded that she understood. I had so many of the classic symptoms: preoccupation with my appearance, frequent examination of myself in the mirror, the belief that others saw my imperfections, frequent cosmetic procedures with little satisfaction, excessive grooming, excessive self-consciousness, refusal to appear in pictures, skin picking, avoidance of social situations and comparing my appearance to others.[1]

While the *what* of BDD seemed clear, the *why* eluded us. It is thought to be caused by a combination of chemical and structural abnormalities in the brain, possible negative environmental factors (triggers) and poor coping skills. Triggers can be a traumatic experience like an accident, a major loss or even an ongoing problem that wears a person down physically or mentally.

I learned that the model most professionals adhere to is predisposition plus triggers, minus coping skills. Good coping skills can mitigate the onset, whereas poor skills can do the opposite. These three factors play out differently in everyone's life. Some people are more resilient and can handle stressors better.

Predisposition has been described as a black hole because it doesn't just involve genetics, but can be based on early childhood experiences and cognitive function as well.

Another person with similar childhood events, personality and chemical makeup like mine wouldn't necessarily have ended up with BDD. Mental illness isn't a given or a choice. Like other illnesses, one can be predisposed

[1] www.mayoclinic.com/health/body-dysmorphic-disorder/

to them, but that alone does not explain the ultimate individual manifestation.

My counselor and I started out talking about how I was feeling at the moment and slowly progressed from there. I needed time to process the place I had come to in life and to build trust with my therapist. Rehashing my history came slowly and painfully, but with a court mandate behind it all and my own need to find some answers, I resigned myself to submit and be engaged in the process.

Over time I understood that my counselor wanted me to try and understand how my past could have played a role in the formation of the mental illness, along with the chemical imbalance in my brain. Our goal was to improve my coping skills for the future.

I began to look at my *ideal* childhood more closely.

My obsession with the mirror started when I was about 15, but as far back as my memory goes, I had always been a neat freak. My siblings had their own compulsions about different things, because OCD and bipolar disorder run in our family. We modeled the poor coping skills of our parents, who learned them from their parents. I chose to be extremely organized and tidy.

I was truly obsessed.

I would watch my mom clean diligently and learn from her, and then I would spend hours straightening my siblings' rooms every week along with my own. If my brother took out a mug and left it sitting on a table for any length of time unattended, I felt compelled to wash it and put it away.

My parents would almost scold me for taking on this role and tried to reassure me that I didn't have to be so overly responsible for everyone's personal belongings, but it must have fed some need inside of me.

It ordered my world.
It gave me a measure of perceived control.

This is typical for coping skills that sort of work in the short-term by offering temporary relief of some anxiety, but can have detrimental consequences down the road.

My hearing impairment played a role, in that it kept me extremely tuned into every visual detail around me, and what I saw either provided peace or panic.

With a history of obsessing over this thing or the next, perfecting my appearance in front of the mirror didn't seem overly unusual. As I began to spend more and more hours looking at myself, consumed with little details, I never thought my behavior odd and, therefore, took no steps to change it.

My parents had their moments of concern over my extreme habits, and looking back they wish they had asked themselves, *"Is this normal?"* The question could have led to some kind of intervention, but instead, my actions just became the norm that everyone got used to. No one gets a manual for parenting someone with a hearing impairment or disability. Most people just try and do the best they can.

My habits and behavior had some of their roots in my disability but I never saw that. Looking back, I began to understand that the reality I lived didn't mirror my friends' and the deficit I felt between everyone else's existence and my own made me feel less lovable, less worthy.

I must have sensed it at some deep level, perhaps unconsciously but it was there, nevertheless, affecting my self-concept and actions.

I was unaware of so much not being able to hear. Looking around I would see dialogue happening everywhere, but I wasn't privy to the nuances that most people took for granted. I had feelings of anxiety and inferiority, scrambling so much to perceive what was happening.

Kids pick up things from hearing others talking and sharing, a wealth of information gleaned that I missed. I didn't know important things like how it is okay for boys to take off their shirts while playing soccer on a hot day, but not okay for girls. I had to learn that one the hard way.

The humiliating way.

Often I would miss a direct question aimed at me and out of sheer embarrassment or in an attempt to not draw attention to my inability to hear, would just say, *"Yes"* or *"Okay."* The puzzled looks and humorous smiles I would receive back clued me in that it hadn't been a yes/no question. Calling myself a dork and laughing it off never really made up for the feelings of shame that lingered. Laughing at myself became a habit and at times, a cover-up.

In my formative years, I wasn't confident that people really liked me. My friends tried to include me in their conversations but I would miss key information, punch lines and their tone of voice. I laughed when they laughed, became serious when they were serious, all the while feeling left out and even worse, not worthy of the time it would take them to rehash it all for me. Looking back I realized that I had never truly been one of them. They would tell me, *"It's okay, Bethany. It wasn't important."*

But it was.

My family members were more sensitized

to these issues, but even they had a hard time including me in every conversation. Driving in the car at night or taking evening walks with a darkening sky kept me out of the loop. Unless my siblings would use little flashlights to light up their lips while they spoke, I was in the dark in more ways than one. The impracticalities of constant inclusion compounded my feelings of isolation and invalidation.

As a teenager, compliments became very meaningful to me. In my insecurity, I clung to my appearance as a way to gain acceptance and I made it a key part of my identity.

And I transferred my obsessive neatness and desire for perfection into the face I saw in the mirror.

By the time I turned 16, my siblings had left home and I had the bathroom all to myself. The perfectionism started with my hair. Having always envied my sister's naturally curly locks, I was often dissatisfied with the in-between wavy version I got stuck with. Before flat irons came on the market, I would take my mom's clothing iron and try to straighten it. The practice became a little dangerous at times trying to set my head on the ironing board and press the steam iron down carefully, the movement away from my scalp to the ends of my hair in order to avoid burning myself.

After going to the salon and getting my

shoulder-length look chopped short, the new cut required even more daily care. My hair is a rich dark brown color and thick. I would get up early, shower, wash my hair, dry it and at this point in my hair history, use a crimper to perfect the look I wanted.

If one little piece looked out of place, I would wash, dry and crimp it all over again: twice, three times, four times.

I would try not to let my frustration and anger further hinder the process but it could take up to three hours to get it right. The satisfaction of finally achieving a perfect look felt great. It diminished the anxiety of not being in control or worthy or lovable.

Then, however, I would go to school and naturally it would get messed up over the course of the day. So the ritual had to start all over again when I got home with more hours wasted in the bathroom. I kind of knew this was extreme behavior, but the need compelled me. I lived for those moments of peace that came when I got it right and stopped the anxious thoughts.

But it didn't stop at my hair. Friends would compliment me on my complexion, telling me I should model skin products because mine looked gorgeous. Nice skin became associated with the perception of my beauty, so any blemish would threaten to make me the ugliest person ever.

If I couldn't get my appearance just right on a given day, I stayed home fretting and stewing, feeling bad about myself from the inside out. Then I would try harder. My life became centered around doing everything in my power:

to make my hair and skin absolutely perfect
to achieve an identity based on perception
to stay in control
to fit in.

The mirror became my constant companion and my dark enemy. The hours I spent in front of it shaped my teenage years and my psychological reality. The image became more and more twisted and my self-perception with it as the hours I stared at it piled up. I began to isolate myself because I thought I didn't look good enough and that I wasn't a likable person that others wanted to be around. I got tired of putting on a happy face and acting like I didn't have any struggles.

My parents would plead with me, exasperated, to get out of the bathroom, but like any slightly rebellious teen, I ignored them and tried to make up excuses for my behavior.

I was alone in my silent world and I didn't want to burden anyone with my problems. As things got more and more horrific with the images in the mirror, my reality became harder to share.

I resolved that I would find a way to cope.
On my own.

And I convinced myself that the mirror didn't lie.

Chapter 9

I used the tools.

Prescription meds were one of the tools in the therapeutic arsenal at the mental health facility. They said it could take two or three months for the psychological medications to really begin to take effect. I certainly didn't feel any less suicidal for what seemed like a very long time. Delving into my past only made it worse and an old addiction kept cropping up: the need to hurt myself.

One of my counselors, Kathy, taught me a safety technique to gauge my negative thinking. We came up with a scale that pinpointed a progression of steps I learned to be aware of. At step two or three I was having trouble sleeping or starting to worry about things. At four or five I was isolating myself and feeling hopeless. At seven or eight I was seeing illusions and thinking destructive thoughts.

My goal was to be at step one but if I got to four or five, it triggered an intervention and I would seek extra counseling to get myself back to a lower number. Controlling my thoughts took on great significance in this process.

The facility had a strict schedule for getting up, eating meals, taking meds and sitting through support groups and classes, all designed to keep us on track and working on our issues. Kathy told me that sometimes the greatest piece of improvement in treatment can come from the smallest of things. There can be a word, concept or idea that sticks and starts a revolutionary change in perception.

The word *hope* became a theme for me. When I would feel sadness and despair coming on, I would come back to that word and anchor myself to it.

One of the most helpful classes for me taught us to live in the moment rather than obsessing over the past or the future. The therapist would place an object in front of us that we had to describe, something round and red, or soft and fuzzy. The exercise made us focus on the here and now rather than worry about what was or what could be, to take control of our thinking in a positive way instead of allowing the bad thoughts to be consuming.

My sessions with my therapist were supposed

to last 15-20 minutes but I found myself hanging out with her longer and freely sharing more and more of my life story. One day I started talking about Taylor and our history poured out of me.

Turning 18 had me graduating from high school and thinking about my future. I was excited to be done with school but a bit envious of my friends who had concrete goals of going on to college and pursuing careers. I couldn't imagine sitting in a classroom for an additional four years with all of my struggles to comprehend dialogue. My options felt limited. I considered finding some kind of training as a cook or maybe pursuing dance, but before my senior year ended this great guy named Taylor came into the picture. Because of him I stopped worrying about some perfect career.

Though he lived in the next resort town over, he had dated one of my best friends when I was a senior. He visited our church one Sunday and ended up getting involved with the worship team. My mom led the team, played the piano and sang. My father finessed the drums. Taylor was the guitarist. They got to know each other well and after he broke up with my classmate, we started a friendship, chatting often via messaging online. His silly sense of humor matched mine and we spent hours sharing life and laughing together.

My senior prom was approaching and I

began thinking about with whom I could go.
My need for attention had me involved with
some rebellious characters at the time, guys
on drugs and in trouble, not suitable for a
nice evening at a Christian school. Sweet
and morally solid Taylor fit the bill perfectly.
I ended up casually mentioning the event in
his hearing, and he jumped right in to ask me
out.

We had a blast and bonded over apple pie
at Denny's into the night hours after the
event. Taylor and I seemed to click at a deep
level, so much so that our relationship got
serious slowly but surely. After the prom we
kept growing as friends for about six months
and then started dating. We shared some
deep things with each other, though I hid my
obsessive tendencies from him, afraid that he
would reject me outright.

Taylor was 6'1" and slightly on the lean side
but toned. Smart, funny, caring, responsible,
a good listener; the list of positive qualities
about him went on and on. With Taylor I felt
beautiful, cherished and free to be myself
in many ways. Sometimes we acted more
like buddies than potential lovers, but the
combination worked.

Being a jokester-kind-of-a-couple more than
a sappy or romantic one fit our personalities,
though Taylor would often buy me flowers.
The notes he chose to accompany them
always made me laugh. It started with a florist

who had a habit of running low on those little preprinted cards with sayings on them. One day he brought me a spring bouquet with a card that said, *"Happy 65th Anniversary!"* followed by a hand-written quip of his own. I looked at him questioningly and he told me with a quick grin that his choices had been limited. It became our thing and I waited with anticipation for the next fun note he would come up with.

Taylor dreamed of flying helicopters, and he was ambitious and hard-working enough to make his dream come true. Needing to make some money for our future, he found a job at a helicopter company doing mechanical work on the machines while taking lessons on the side. My parents' home was closer to work than his own, so he built a room in their garage and spent a lot of nights there.

Taylor's grandparents owned a resort in a nearby town and I spent the following summer working there doing a variety of jobs. I tried waitressing, but it turns out the ability to hear is sort of mandatory for getting the orders right. Reading lips can only take a person so far. One day a customer asked for a Kokanee Beer. Not being knowledgeable enough about beer to understand the nuances of those mouthed words, I went up to the bar and put in an order for a *coconut beer*. Phil, the bartender, looked at me suspiciously and said, *"What?"* Not deterred, I insisted he pour me a coconut beer. After showing me the label, we both got a good chuckle out of my mix-up.

I got transferred to the kitchen pretty quickly after that and was much happier for it. But of course, *Coconut* became my nickname for the rest of the summer.

Taylor proposed on Christmas Eve with family all around us. We had been going around sharing individually about the things we were thankful for. When it was Taylor's turn he said, *"I am thankful for my beautiful girlfriend. I love her."* Then he got down on one knee with a gorgeous diamond ring in hand and asked me to be his wife. It truly surprised me. I started crying and gave him an exuberant, "Yes!"

Jumping up to share my joy with everyone, I felt this little trickle run down my nose. Of all times to get a bloody nose. I ended up in the family photo album with my head thrown back to stop the bleeding and my ring raised high in front of me, still managing to gaze admiringly at my sparkling hand in the overhead light, a delighted smile on my face.

We got married a year later on New Year's Day at the church of my childhood. Our pastor performed the ceremony and we held the reception in the basement hall decorated in a winter wonderland theme. We had fake snow, a little ice skating rink replete with a meandering bridge over it, and a sleigh for the wedding gifts perched on the far end.

My dress was white with sequined spaghetti straps attached to a square neckline that shaped down to a "v" at my waist. From there it flared out to almost cover my feet adorned in pretty glass-like slippers. I wore a tiara with a veil cascading down my back. My bridesmaids wore sleeveless velvety maroon gowns that fell gracefully to the floor.

Right before it was time to head upstairs from our changing room, a friend brought in a big vase of roses from my groom. I eagerly grabbed the little card to see what kind of mischief he was up to. The card read: *"Congratulations. It's a Boy!"*

On the bottom he had tacked on: *"...who can't wait to marry you."*

The unexpected sappiness brought tears that I couldn't hide and a lengthy explanation to my attendants of why it was the sweetest moment of the day.

Not being restful beach people, Taylor and I chose Las Vegas for our honeymoon so we could have an adventure any hour of the day or night. A roller coaster ride at 3:00 in the morning suited us perfectly. It didn't matter that we were too young to legally gamble or imbibe alcohol because that really wasn't our scene. We bought tickets to fun shows and lived up the Vegas nightlife in our own way.

Upon returning to Idaho and settling into the domestic realm, I decided to quit working, which gave me hours and hours of free time. Wanting to be a good wife, I cooked, cleaned and took care of the details of our lives. When Taylor tried to help with domestic duties, my obsessive-compulsive issues caused me to redo all of his housekeeping efforts, but he put up with my quirky behavior. He remained faithful and loyal through the slow unveiling of my problems.

My quirkiness, however, kept getting worse and worse.

I bought new clothes but couldn't bring myself to wear them, not feeling pretty enough or worthy to put them on. I began to spend my days in grungy sweats and old t-shirts, my hair in a pony-tail and baseball cap. I felt like I looked disgusting, so why should I bother?

Taylor would try to get me to wear something nice to go out to dinner, saying I was beautiful, wanting to encourage me. I would get defensive and tell him to stop pushing me. He would drop it for a while, but the oddity of him being the only one to ever put on nice clothes for an outing or an event continued to pop up between us. It caused tension that I couldn't ease. With time I balked at going anywhere, preferring to stay home and avoid social contact.

With all of the free time I had to focus on

myself, my BDD symptoms worsened rapidly. I cannot recount the hours I spent in the bathroom. I would pull out one piece of hair and another and another, pick at spots on my face until they bled severely, file my teeth with emery boards to make them look more even. Makeup seemed useless to help my appearance, so in a fit of frustration, I threw it all away. As much as I tried, nothing could make me look better or fix my face.

I kept the shades closed all day wherever we were living, so as not to get a glimpse of myself in some reflection that could catch me unaware. It unnerved me too greatly. The times I stared at myself had to be intentional and controlled.

I would gaze at the mirror and tell myself: *"Bethany, you are worthless. You are ugly. Why are you still here?"* This is when I first began to see distorted images of my face, creepy and terrible, like it was moving and melting before my eyes. Tears were an everyday occurrence and depression gripped me, but I hid most of it, not wanting to be a burden on anyone, especially not my newly wed husband.

We moved around a lot the first few years of our marriage. My obsession with my body moved too. I focused attention on my arms one week and the next on my neck and chest. It wasn't that the skin on them was particularly ugly, but any little fleck or discoloration made me think there were crawly things inside my skin trying to force their way out. So I had to find a way to pick and purge them from my body.

With all of these things consuming me, I began to hate my life, and hurting myself became an outlet for my anger. In the process I became addicted to pain.

I bought facial kits online that contained strong ingredients. The packages warned of the dangers of leaving the product on too long. They advised the use of a fan in a well-ventilated room and only using the chemicals for a minute or two, but I would leave them on my face for an hour or more. I loved the feeling of the burn. My face would look badly sunburned afterward, which I would have to make up excuses for. I would give my face a chance to heal and then do it all over again, craving that sensation. A lot of the peels I found weren't strong enough, so I constantly searched for something more toxic.

When we lived with Taylor's mom for a while in a remodeled section of her basement, the tools on the workbench down there drew me.

Not to build or repair anything.
But as weapons of self-destruction.

My favorite was the electric sander. I would use it on my face until it became raw and bleeding. The best tool for my upper chest was one of those paint scraper brushes with thick metal prongs. The frenzied pain I inflicted helped to relieve pent up feelings, but like my other obsessions, the satisfaction it provided lasted only briefly.

I tried to hide my wounds and would make up excuses for my injured body when someone noticed. But once in a while I would confess to my husband that I had had a bad day and deliberately inflicted damage. A couple of times I even admitted that seeing a kitchen knife made me want to really hurt myself. Appalled and concerned, he urged me to get help.

I saw a therapist for a while, but she didn't have a diagnosis for me beyond OCD, and her only advice was for me to wear gloves full-time so I couldn't touch my face. I went on a psych medication and it did help a bit with the OCD and the length of time in the bathroom, but not enough in my estimation. Like a lot of people on medications for psychological issues, once a person feels a little bit better, he or she can wrongly conclude they are no longer necessary, when just the opposite is true.

Taylor tried to help me manage the obsessions. We covered the bathroom mirror so I couldn't spend hours in front of it, but of course I would just uncover it. For the next attempt, he took down the mirror and hid it offsite where I couldn't find it. After

two days I became desperate without my
fix, and rummaged through old boxes in the
garage until I found a little half-broken one.
In the end we decided that ridding our lives of
mirrors just wasn't practical for either of us, or
any real solution to my problems.

Not having an accurate diagnosis, coupled with
not being given the right medication, caused
me to experience little improvement over the
next year. Still hating myself, I figured there
wasn't any more help to be found. I stopped
taking the med and believed it was up to me
to keep trying to fix my problems on my own,
without those seemingly useless therapeutic
tools.

And not knowing any better, I clung to that
belief.

Bethany's Family Pictures

Bethany with Dad and Mom (Joe and Nancy, 1982)

Willow, Bethany and Abe on Grandma Edie's beach.

Bethany in the 5th grade.

Bethany (far right) age 14 with her dance team.

Bethany
and Willow
pretending
to be
supermodels.

High School
Graduation

Class of 2000

The sisters at Willow's college graduation party.

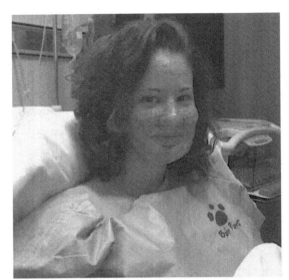

Bethany in the hospital prepping for first surgery.

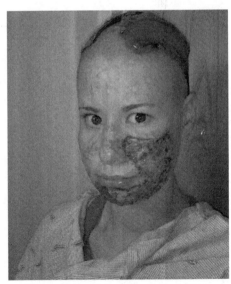

They shaved Bethany's hair to use the skin of her scalp.

Willow's wedding with Bethany as Maid of Honor. A typical pose found them laughing together. This is the last picture taken of the two sisters before the injury.

Chapter 10

I made plans.

My story with Taylor kept unfolding as I shared deeper things with my counselor.

My unhappiness grew and grew with him, with all my issues and with my life. I never questioned his love, but I wondered what it would be like to live on my own and enjoy a measure of freedom I had never experienced being married at such a young age. I felt trapped by circumstances, not the least of which was my own dysfunction. Some other life called to me, one that would fill this gaping hole of depression and dreadful feelings that I experienced every day.

I was tired of fighting the image in the mirror, hiding my struggles and trying to be a good wife when I knew my inadequacies on too many levels. Just like having those new clothes but never feeling good enough about myself to wear them, I had this deep sense that I wasn't good enough for Taylor and never would be.

A typical weekend for us could never just be about living life together or doing anything spontaneous without my OCD and BDD interfering.

Not ever.

We would get up Saturday morning, and knowing how long it would take for me to get ready, Taylor would grab me a coffee and then go to work for several hours. I would text him when I was ready to officially start the day. Once we met up again later in the afternoon, we would walk our dog, run errands and usually have a nice dinner out somewhere.

How I spent those early hours is part of the life I hid for the seven years of our marriage. When we eventually moved into our own home about year number three, my obsessive tendencies kicked up a notch.

On average it took me four hours to clean our small apartment every day. I started in the bedroom making the bed, picking up, dusting and vacuuming. Then I would tackle the bathroom and clean the toilet, shower, sink, floor and mirror, making them spotless. On to the living room I went with the same routine and then to the kitchen.

Once the basic cleaning was done, I went back into each room and tackled drawers, closets, baskets and bins. To get sidetracked by a wayward thought or lose focus compelled me to start a task all over again. Every detail had to be just so. Once I finished the cleaning and straightening, I then headed to the mirror to work on my appearance, taking up more chunks of time obsessing over this and that.

Every day.

Heaven help me if I had an 8:00 a.m. appointment somewhere. That meant my day started at 5:00 a.m. or earlier to get it all done.

Twice a week I cleaned out the fridge. For most people that would mean purging anything with green growth on it. For me it meant removing all items and washing down each shelf and crevice. I washed a load of cleaning rags every day and used copious bottles of dish soap.

My husband and I often ate dinner out to avoid the time I would have to spend cleaning after preparing the meal. Some days it was just easier to ignore my behavior and find ways around it, both of us trying to cope and maintain some semblance of a normal life together.

At other times we would sit down and make a list of the absolute essential things for me to do, with the goal of cutting out the obsessive ones. It gave me permission to reduce and manage my OCD, but the results were always temporary. This cyclical pattern of making a plan, failing to follow it, crying out to Taylor and making a new plan only perpetuated itself.

The reality was that in the end I sabotaged my marriage, being helpless to change my thinking and actions. The need to escape seemed logical at the time. My unhappiness and frustration with myself made me want to change my life in some drastic way, but I didn't know which direction help lay in.

Taylor could see me slowly drifting away emotionally, apathetic and so unhappy. He would look at me with the pain of the world in his eyes. I hated hurting him and it only added to my sense of guilt, the need to punish myself and somehow escape my life. We talked about getting some counseling together, but never acted upon the thought. That was the start of our relationship splintering.

The day I asked for a divorce will stay in my mind forever. We had been married for seven years. He cried when I told him what I wanted and simply asked, *"Why?"* His loyalty through so much staggered me. I had no answer, just a wrenching certainty that I had to get out, that I was not enough, pushing him away in the process.

Taylor wanted to give me more time to

make sure of my decision, so we made up a separation plan that would leave the door open in case I changed my mind. He had lined up a job in another city for a six-month stint. I could have gone with him and lived in a hotel, but instead the plan became that I would stay with some family members in Idaho. It would give me time to really think things through.

That time away from each other only confirmed my warped plan. That cocktail of BDD, depression and OCD was ruling my life and destroying all sound reasoning.

Neither one of us had told anyone of our separation, but the family began to guess, seeing our odd behavior and living arrangements.

Divorcing him made me happy for about two seconds. The regrets rolled in almost immediately. My life and issues took a dreadful turn for the worse.

Within a couple of months I was actively trying to get him back, texting him often. My pleading would be something like: *"I'm so sorry. I made a big mistake. Can we work something out?"* He would write back different thoughts but all with one theme and not the answer I wanted to hear: *"I don't think I can do it. I need time. I am really hurt."*

But those words actually preserved a bit of hope in my heart, so I kept texting, almost begging at times but my desperation must have appeared extremely unhealthy.

And it was.

I knew he felt bitter that I had walked away, and with time, he probably also realized what a dysfunctional life we had been living, and was wary of stepping back into that old regime. Nothing had changed about me. I couldn't blame him.

So I had to let him go.

Back at the mental health facility, my counselor talked me through the regret and heartache. I certainly hadn't gotten over him or worked through the grief, let alone my depression. It had been a major trigger for my suicide attempt. Through counseling I let myself begin to feel the pain of that loss and it caused me to make some additional plans, but not of the constructive variety.

After two months at the facility my suicidal tendencies had quieted. The staff safely let me have a razor to shave my legs at this point and other self-care tools that I might have used for another attempt earlier. But my desire for self-punishment and the need to have my feelings jumpstarted hadn't quite gone away. That craving for pain had been steadily creeping back up on me.

I had new reasons to punish myself: the pain

I had caused my family and friends, lying to the world by blaming an imaginary minority woman, the financial expense of needing medical attention and psychological help. Those were my excuses for the destructive plan I then carried out.

Outings were allowed from the facility and I commandeered a couple of friends I had made there to help. I donned a hooded sweatshirt, oversized jacket and glasses thinking to disguise myself. We drove to the very same hardware store from the past and walked in. I handed one of my friends the money and sent her to the far back where I knew they shelved the acid. I wandered around the front of the store, trying to look as inconspicuous as possible, a difficult task with my scarred face and furtive glances.

My friend paid for the drain cleaner and we walked out. Feelings of triumph filled me as we drove away, and selfishly, I wasn't thinking about the other occupants of the car and how I was using them. They hadn't put together the reason for buying the acid, as mystifying as that sounds with all the media attention that had surrounded me. I had chosen friends to help who were as messed up as myself and unable to connect the dots of my behavior.

Back at the facility, I hid the bottle outside under a bush with the plan to sneak out in the evening to retrieve it. Several hours later it was sitting on my dresser as I perched on my bed anticipating the pain to come. My arms and legs were the target.

The pain called to me.

I glanced at my phone and saw a slew of missed calls from my mom. I then knew she knew. And shaking my head in disbelief, I wondered how. As it turned out, the manager of the hardware store had recognized me and genuinely concerned, had called the police. They had showed up at my parents' door to let them know. My mom had frantically tried to get ahold of me and when I hadn't answered, called the mental health facility. The staff came to my door knocking: *"Bethany, your mother called us. We know you have the drain cleaner. Are you okay?"*

I opened the door, regretfully and mournfully having to relinquish my prize, my thoughts whirling.

But something clicked. Whether it was my mom's tears or my own, I looked at the plans I had made and was finally and rightfully beginning to be horrified. Reality began to sink into my thought processes and that evening marked a slow but sure turning point. I went back to my friends and apologized for putting them in such an untenable position of helping me buy my *fix.*

That incident fueled my need to get to the bottom of why these behaviors continued to drive me. I finally saw how irrational they truly were.

My sister's words came back to me from the providential text I had ignored that day in my truck with the acid: *"For some reason I just feel like I need to text you and tell you that you don't have to punish yourself. We love you. God loves you. Just the way you are."*

And I made the words linger.

I didn't have to punish myself.
My family loved me.
God loved me.
Just the way I was.

Chapter 11

I got rid of stuff.

My counseling sessions at the mental health facility continued to glean insights.

All those hours as a child, teenager and young adult that I had spent straightening every object, gadget, piece of clothing and carton of food, arranging and rearranging, caused me to look at possessions differently as my mental illness progressed. It got so tiring that I became a minimalist. After all, the less you have, the less you have to obsess over.

Unfortunately, minimalism can be an obsession too.

During the last couple of years with Taylor, giving things away became a compulsion. He would head out to work in the morning and return later in the day to find items missing. One night he sat down on the couch with his usual soft drink and leaned to the left to set it down, only to find the small side table gone. *"What happened to the table?"* he suspiciously asked. I lied and said I didn't like that one and was planning to buy something different.

I mostly purged his stuff, of course, because he had boxes of it in the garage and our closets, something I never allowed in my own life. There were old clothes, letters, video tapes and books that I deemed *excessive junk*. I slowly gave away our silverware and extra dishes too. With just the two of us, why did we need ten forks? Taylor knew about my purging obsession and he would be upset at times, especially when it involved his possessions. He asked me to stop and I would try for a while, but the need to purge stuff built back up and the craving wouldn't leave me.

I would throw good food away to keep the fridge from being cluttered. Shopping for groceries every day enabled me to have the exact number of items for each meal, with no more and no less, another obsessive endeavor of mine. I couldn't close the door until I got it just right.

My pantry was a work of art from an organizer's viewpoint, every can and container neatly aligned and standing proud. I developed a technique for folding down the top of a bag of chips that defied gravity, or whatever it is that makes those unruly items flop open constantly.

Thinking through these patterns in counseling gave me a picture of deeper *stuff* I needed to get rid of and make sense out of. As the anti-depressant medication began to work and as I spent long hours talking at the mental health facility, I began to deal with the load I was carrying psychologically.

There were burdens I had never gone through and purged: the weight of my disability and control issues from the past. They had built up over so many years of trying to cope on my own instead of getting real help with my mental illness. The first step was to own that illness and not try to hide it away in some far recess of my psyche or in an organized refrigerator or perfectly cleaned rooms.

I knew that I couldn't completely purge BDD, OCD and depression from my life but maybe I could find a way to manage them, even minimize them. I began to more honestly sift through the junk, sharing and journaling the things that held me back, the pain I had refused to acknowledge, the hurts I carried and had buried.

My family had a history of psychological issues. My sister, who is over six feet tall, struggled intensely with an eating disorder in college. At one point she only weighed 100 pounds. For her it was about control as well, wanting to have the perfect outer appearance that would gain her approval and acceptance. Anorexia is often linked with BDD. After my suicide attempt, the signs of my mental illness that she had missed became clear to her. She felt like she should have seen it all playing out and intervened.

We have relatives on both sides of the family who suffer from depression, bipolar disorder and obsessive-compulsive behaviors. Whatever combination of genes I inherited, there were tendencies ingrained in my DNA since birth. Growing up without the ability to hear greatly affected my concept of self and how I interacted with the world. But even without a hearing impairment, I probably would have struggled with some type of psychological distress.

As it was, the constant battle to glean information from lips, body language and other cues because I couldn't hear, consumed my mind with the external. I learned to look outwardly for approval and based my self-concept on what others thought of me. Fitting in was extra difficult and so I tried harder to be what I presumed others wanted me to be in the family, at school and at church.

I tried to be perfect.

I joked, gave encouraging words and smiled to gain attention and friends. Everyone finds a way to make life work, to their own hurt at times, and my path seemed to afford me what

I sought. I was popular, though I paid a price for it.

Those rebellious guys I dated in high school used me, though I was using them as well. I traded my body for their status because it elevated mine. I traded my self-esteem and respect, in a sense to be arm candy. But in my desperation to be somebody at the time, it felt right. My church and family required higher standards for my behavior that were good and healthy, but I conveniently ignored them. It was my life and rebelliously I maneuvered to find a way to be somebody in the world's eyes.

Looking perfect became one of my worst obsessions and focusing on the outer kept my focus off of looking at my motivations and my heart. My dad would often try to build me up saying things like, *"B, you are funny and you have a beautiful heart. You attract people. They love to be around you because you make them feel good. You make your mother and I so proud."*

Who wouldn't love to hear that from their parents and be blessed by it? But I never felt worthy of those compliments, never absorbed them into my identity or gleaned encouragement from them. I dismissed everyone's opinion but my own warped one.

My perception that I looked defective never got challenged in my thinking because of the BDD. What had looked like vanity, spending so much time in front of the mirror, actually had been the mental illness playing itself out. The perception of my face had been askew, not the reality.

My journal entries at the mental health facility became a mix of despair and hope as I continued to sift through the wreckage of my life:

> "Tonight as I lay in bed, many things are going through my head – who am I and who could I be? I think of what has happened to me. What is the life I am living? All these things I am thinking out loud. My head hurts from thoughts of hurting myself. I pace the room, walking in circles. All these questions I want answers to. I can never seem to pay attention to finishing a simple task. My heart hurts and it is beating fast. Where did I go wrong? I cry.
>
> Why? I ask. Why me? I think of all the negative things I thought. This is not the real me. It just can't be. Laying in my bed I begin to have hope and smile instead. Letting go of all my stress, I see what the Lord has given me. Feeling all the pain, I begin to let it out from holding all this guilt.
>
> Back to sleep I go as I cry, thinking about how hard it had been. Thinking just how hard, I try and see that I am

*on my way to hope. Will do good and
hope for the best. God will take care
of the rest. The many things that I will
achieve. I know I can succeed.*

*Back to sleep I go, trying to stop the
rushing thoughts..."*

Some days I became too tired to dig further,
but I resolved to not give up, knowing the
consequences of all that had transpired and
needing a better future. I gained hope as I
saw the medication working. I was crying out
for it, needing to experience some relief from
the obsessions that had controlled me for so
long.

I longed to be rid of them and to discover
the real Bethany, to take those scattered bits
and pieces and finally make them into some
cohesive whole. I wanted to be a person
able to relate to the world from a position of
strength rather than constant weakness, and
to value the Bethany that my parents saw.

My life was not a piece of excess junk to be
carelessly tossed in the give-away bin.

Chapter 12

I hit bottom.

After making the decision to divorce Taylor, I moved to live with a friend in Spokane. My soon-to-be ex-husband showed up one day as we had agreed upon, knocking on my door. I opened it to see him standing there looking so handsome and strong, resignation and deep sadness in his eyes. He mumbled one phrase, *"Are you ready?"* and we left, hardly conversing as we drove to the courthouse, both of us feeling numb. We simply filled out the paperwork together, filed it and said goodbye. The tears wouldn't stop that day.

My behavior mirrored my inner pain in the weeks and months to come. I racked up credit card debt, gained weight and desperately sought attention from new men.

Needing a job to support myself, the search led me to a part-time care-taking position for several handicapped clients. Once again I was left with many hours at home alone and performing destructive acts to hurt myself.

After reading comments from women online about how bad the sting of laser treatments felt, I became fascinated with their pain potential. I made an appointment for a consultation and practically had to beg the doctor to work on a face that didn't appear to need the treatment. I paid a lot of money, only to be disappointed by the low level of pain the laser actually inflicted.

The friend I was living with became concerned after observing my lifestyle and one day mentioned a few things to my sister, hinting that I wasn't in a good place. My family immediately made contact and asked me to come to Vancouver. I had been planning to move closer to them eventually but was also dreading it. They loved Taylor so much and my actions had broken their hearts too.

After listening to much pleading from them, I decided to take their advice and move home. Though I tried to hold it together on my own with family near, my self-destructive behavior kept slowly progressing all the way up to the day I bought the acid. I wish I hadn't been so good at hiding things.

Job-hunting seemingly consumed all of my time and I rarely opened up about anything. Worrying about being a burden to my parents,

I scrambled to socialize a bit, help pay the bills and keep my depression at bay. My family saw I was struggling and wanted to be there for me but I shut them out over and over. Until that day in the jail when the truth finally came out, they had no idea how terrible my inner world had become.

Because this first time that I hit bottom had ended in such tragedy, I had a desperate hope that the second time would have a better outcome.

Halfway through my year at the mental health facility marked the lowest point in my recovery. I truly hit rock bottom. And I saw my behavior so differently. With the medication working, I was thinking and feeling clearly for maybe the first time in my life.

My actions overwhelmed me. I would sit for hours and remember what I had done to myself. I looked in the mirror every day and could hardly believe what I saw, my beautiful complexion that used to bring me compliments now marred.

At first we all thought my face would heal well, though it was taking its time to close all of the wounds. The damaged areas started out looking splotchy, like a flat road rash, but then I began to notice blister-like puffs of red appearing. The scars seemed to grow daily. My burn surgeon recommended that I wear a plastic mask to attempt to reduce the scarring.

I broke down when he told me about the mask, knowing that I would have to commit to wearing it twenty-some hours every day and that it would consume my life for a year or more. Needing encouragement, I asked my family and the staff at the facility to monitor me, to make sure I wore the mask as prescribed. It took a couple of weeks to get used to the tight fit, the uncomfortable straps across my hair, the feeling of slight suffocation it gave me.

My original burn surgeon told me honestly that I would never get back the face I used to have. Back in my little room at the mental health facility, I sat with that, feeling numb and hopeless. I didn't see much point in going on with my life, but I didn't come up with a suicide plan either. I vowed to give myself some time.

My old enemy, the mirror, tripped me up a few times at the facility, but now I was fighting new demons rather than the old. Looking into the reasons behind it all brought up a lot of emotion. Some days I would lock the bathroom door and stare at my face for long minutes, berating myself for how hideous I now looked and ignoring the knocks of other residents needing to get in there.

I would stand with my new image before me, silently venting my anger both at myself and at my burn surgeon for *letting* my face get this bad. I knew he didn't deserve the blame but anger isn't always rational. My venting would turn to bitter tears that could have flooded the place.

My beautiful skin.
Gone.
No way to reverse the damage.

A few times I took a washcloth and scrubbed brutally at the awful scars. I screamed in my head for them to be gone, but the abuse only made them more angry and red.

Now that I was thinking more logically because of my counseling and the medication, I realized that my behavior was destructive and I forced myself to stop. That imagined distorted face in the mirror that had haunted me for so long, in part had become a reality. And I had to live with the fact that my actions caused it to happen. It was a lot to stomach.

If only there was a way to turn back the clock.

One day I wrote out a list of regrets for all that had transpired. I wished I could take back those wasted hours in the bathroom as a teenager that fueled my obsession. I wished I had lived on my own for a while before getting married, gotten psychological help and entered the union with a healthier sense of self. I wished the word divorce had never left my lips, that I hadn't hurt Taylor. I wished I could undo the damage I had done to myself physically, and the pain I caused myself and all the people who truly loved me. I wished I could undo the lies I told to deceive the world.

If only I hadn't been so stubborn to think I was capable of getting better on my own.

If only I hadn't clung to the belief that my life was a burden to others if I shared my struggles.

If only I had known that my problem had a medical name and real treatment options.

I wrote these regrets and more down on paper and sought forgiveness from my Father in heaven who adores me more than my earthly dad. Burning the list seemed symbolic, giving me a picture of pain and sin wiped out.

My sin and my pain.
Truly forgiven and truly redeemed.
The idea seemed miraculous.

The interesting thing about hitting bottom is that one's world levels out. The storm has to blow itself out eventually. I couldn't go back and change anything, only forward.

I had no idea what my life was going to look like or what I was going to look like in the end, but even with only vague hopes and dreams, something above and beyond all of this kept calling to me.

Chapter 13

I began to see.

The need to appear a second time at court, six months after the first one, menaced my conscious thoughts. I was crawling my way out from hitting bottom, the scars on my face weren't getting any better and the thought of going to jail still frightened me.

My lawyers had been working hard sifting through the evidence for my defense. We hoped to get a reduction in the theft counts in light of my mental state and the harm I had done to myself. These consequences I would have to live with for the rest of my life, temporary incarceration paling in comparison.

As the date of the court appearance drew closer, my anxiety spiraled. I was afraid of the verdict, the reactions of the crowd, the aftermath. My tears flowed freely. I was crying for the grief in me and for all the unknown.

But the difference this time around was my perception.

Whereas before I felt alone in my struggles and a burden to everyone, now I chose to let myself feel the love and care from people surrounding me. I took in their comfort and words of encouragement, and drew strength from it.

A journal entry from this time shows my mindset:

> "I want to be encouraged today.
> If and when I am down in depression,
> if my heart is broken, and my life is
> in such disarray that I have become
> lost on life's journey, I can put my
> hope in God and He will bring me
> through. With faith... I will make it
> through."

My perception also differed regarding my sense of reality and self-awareness. They had shifted dramatically with those months at the mental health facility, and my coping strategies had improved greatly. Being in a place where other people struggled with some of the same manifestations of mental illness that I did made me look at my life in a new way. I would watch the guy next to me raking his nails clear through the skin on his arm, and with a sigh of exasperation think it was foolish, pointless and destructive. And then it would hit me that I did that too.

My fellow strugglers taught me a lot. We learned together how to manage our anxiety, deal with panic attacks and work out conflict in healthier ways. I saw better means of coping and navigating through the tough spots.

We were rebuilding our broken lives. Together.

I had a long way to go to overcome my issues, but for the first time I had hope for a new beginning. Dwelling in the trenches of mental illness is a hard, demanding place to learn about life, but the results are tenacious and deeply felt. Thus, my fear of it all going away with a severe verdict went deep.

My lawyers advised me to write a letter to the community and express any thoughts I wanted to convey. They also convinced me to give a short interview after the verdict to a local paper. I walked into the courtroom feeling like a different person from the one who had entered only a few short months before. My world had tilted and I wanted to make things right as much as possible. I had felt bad all along for my behavior and deception, but now my life mattered to me, and my reputation with it. I wondered if I could ever rebuild that and take back my name from the scandal seemingly forever doomed to surround it.

The hearing lasted only a few minutes. My

lawyers had come to an agreement with the prosecutor beforehand, agreeing to reduce the charges because of my mental state and lack of real intent to steal.

The judge decided to give me a suspended one-year sentence for the misdemeanor crime of making false statements to a public official. I also had to pay back $3982.46 in overtime salaries for the police department. Regarding the three counts of second-degree theft, the lawyers reached a plea bargain to drop two of them. The third felony count would be taken off my record upon completion of an 18-month diversion program involving continued psychological care and 240 hours of community service.

My lawyers fought for a form of community service that would be a good match for me. The thought of cleaning highways with traffic whipping by frightened me. I didn't even like to ride my bike around the neighborhood with cars driving here and there. Without the ability to hear them coming up on me, it felt too risky. The fact that I had more leeway to choose community service projects that would fit my disability greatly relieved me.

I had written a long apology to the African American community, my church and my friends. Sadly, it ended up getting shortened and somewhat impersonalized for the courtroom version. I felt nervous and shaky giving my statement, standing before everyone in the silent courtroom. My lawyers positioned themselves on either side of me, lending me emotional support. I felt God watching out for me as well, His presence tangible as I listened to the judge and answered his questions.

It helped to see compassion in his eyes as he said: *"The community is getting paid back... I do think it puts Ms. Storro in the position of helping herself."* And then his eyes fell directly on me: *"I wish you the best of luck. You have a lot hanging over your head."*

Barely holding back tears, I nodded and agreed to the final verdict laid out before me, thankful that prison and an extended trial would be avoided, thankful for his kind words. My lawyers represented me with such diligence and compassion, wanting what was best for me rather than what would further their own careers, another enormous gift I was thankful for.

Afterwards, I told a local reporter a bit more about BDD in an interview and thanked everyone for letting me share some of my story.

I expected people to be harsh and dissolved in tears when I read a few compassionate comments online from the interview article. One woman's statement particularly touched me:

"Bethany was mentally unstable and is now getting help. When you take a look at her face the evidence is clear as the plastic she wears, that she sentenced herself to life-long disfigurement. Time in jail or any other sentence would not come close to the punishment she inflicted upon herself. Yes, Jesus loves her... when we were yet sinners, He died for us. He didn't give his life for the pure and whole ones. He gave a GIFT of new life to the broken ones. Bethany was broken; just like the rest of us."[1]

I felt that brokenness, but also a humbleness and appreciation for those grace-filled words. The papers had never reported that I was hearing impaired and dealing with BDD, as well as issues from my past. My journey was long and complex and I hadn't been in a place to share much of it until this point. I had hope that people would see my story differently once I could communicate it, but mental illness is tough to understand, and my not telling the truth is unforgivable in some people's eyes.

And though I was seeing everything more clearly, as the judge inferred, it was still going to take far-seeing eyes to navigate the long road ahead of me.

---

[1] http://columbian.com/news/2011/apr/08/live-blog

Chapter 14

I began to truly hear.

Perfectionism. It was a shadow over my life that had controlled it for so long and in so many ways. I thought if I were perfect, then I would be loved and given the attention I craved.

My skin.
My relationships.
My world.

The illusions of perfection came not only in the mirror, but also in thinking this was the path to happiness and satisfaction in life.

And I know that I am not alone.

Our culture expects people to perform well and it worships a very outward idea of beauty. Anyone outside of the norm is put at a disadvantage, subtly or blatantly.

In my formative years, I remember hearing friends around me criticize actors for the cosmetic surgery craze and I would outwardly agree, but inside I thought otherwise. I wanted the ability to improve my appearance. I longed for smiles and the attention of men and the route to that end seemed clear back then: perfect beauty.

I have been asked how I thought damaging my face could gain me a new and improved one. Working with damaged tissue is nothing like working with the healthy version. Cosmetic surgery, the nipping and tucking kind, works for pliable skin. Scar tissue is completely different and often unmanageable, something I have learned through this process.

My answer is that I never expected a different face from the acid because I hadn't counted on living. I didn't damage it to make it better. I angrily just wanted it gone, grasping nothing beyond the goal of self-destruction.

I hurt myself because I craved the pain.
To try and end the obsession.
To not feel so dead inside.
To be punished.

No one is perfect or can be perfect. I grew up in a church that talked about forgiveness, grace and a loving Jesus who literally took the punishment that I deserved for my sins.

I believed it on the surface, but needed to let those truths sink deeper into my life.

My bondage to the lie of perfectionism revealed itself in my rebellious teenage years, the hours in front of the mirror, the craving to get out of my marriage because I didn't think I was good enough, hurting myself over and over and in the lies I told. That bondage caused me to want to end my life because I saw no hope or future for it.

Through the aftermath of my suicide attempt, that shadow of bondage is slowly lifting. There is freedom in admitting that I have a mental illness requiring long-term medication, supervision and help from professionals. There is freedom in the realization that I do not have to be perfect. I can't be. It is no longer my goal in life. I am forgiven. I have a Savior who is the only perfect One. I don't have to whip myself into shape or change the basics of who I am.

Now my focus is building my identity in healthy ways and discovering the real Bethany, who is trying not to be a slave to the outward any longer. I tell myself this every day, and I allow my family and friends to encourage the process.

I confess that I am not there yet. Obsessive-compulsive tendencies hover and I fight to be organized to a certain degree and then let go. I am experimenting with techniques to control my thinking and behavior, to use healthy coping strategies.

When I am standing in front of my bathroom mirror, I try to remember to set the timer on my phone to only allow myself a set number of minutes for grooming. When I find myself checking something over and over, I say a phrase out loud to signal the task is truly complete, something like: *"No. I'm done. Time to move on."*

A baby step for my minimalist tendencies is to place a new object on my desk, maybe even two, and then not touch them for a few days. It is monumentally difficult to not rearrange them. I have to battle a craving to put them away, out of sight. Just letting them sit there taunts me, but the victory comes when I shrug off their power over me.

I don't have many clothes in my closet yet, but eventually I plan to buy a couple of nice outfits and actually wear them. One of my survivor friends gave me a piece of advice she had gotten along her journey: a woman living with scars can benefit from being well-groomed. A nice outfit can balance out the negative attention and helps to convey a sense of confidence with oneself.

It seems contradictory to be playing the culture game of having to look good, but the reality is we live in this world and have to function in it to a certain degree. I don't have to be obsessed with my appearance but I can still show that I care about myself and feel content with who I am as a person.

Having never lived with the thought of balance in my life, these concepts are new to me and I feel like I am making new discoveries every day about how to be and think. I am trying to really listen to the advice given to me by people with wisdom, move forward and live in a healthy way, and to take care of myself emotionally.

Admittedly, I am still not comfortable being in crowds or in front of people. Social withdrawal, a side effect of BDD, keeps me isolated and too self-focused. I hope that will change as I continue to get more in touch with myself and risk getting back out there, building relationships and loving others. I want to convey a sense of confidence some day, so people may see how far I have come, and maybe find hope for their own compulsions and issues.

For so long, I concealed my reality from friends and loved ones, and suffered the loneliness of that. Hiding is what got me in so much trouble. Writing this book is my declaration that I don't want to hide anymore. I have not told my story to get attention (heaven knows I have had more attention than any person with social anxiety can handle), but rather to try and move on with my life, to get out of the shadows.

It seemed my existence was all about me before. I want that to change, for my focus to be more outward. The friends I made at the mental health facility showed me a side to life that I never knew existed apart from my own scarred journey. Many people suffer from mental illness. I can identify it in others much more easily now because I know the signs and have experienced the gamut of unhealthy coping strategies people use to try and resolve their illnesses alone.

On my own road to hope, perhaps I can tug some fellow strugglers along with me who are barely aware that they need it.

I hear them better now.

Afterword

Facing the truth about myself has been no easy task. So often the feelings get in the way.

Grief and joy.

How does one get a handle on them and balance the two? After the suicide attempt, I changed my name to Bethany Joy, mostly to avoid negative recognition. But it also played into my new goal, to live being in touch with my feelings in an honest and healthy way. I hid for too long. Even from myself.

Mostly from myself.

I had only played at joy with that shadow over my life for so many years. The jokes I cracked and smiles I gave were so often based on my need to be liked, rather than coming from a joyful or content place inside. So much of my past involved covering up negative emotions.

I didn't know the Bethany I saw looking in the mirror, constantly operating out of a sense of lack. Those monstrous images that plagued me, my face eerily melting in front of me, had given me no sense of the real picture. Though the mirror is no longer spouting lies to me, scars have become my new reality. But I deem reality better than lies. Catching a glimpse of myself passing by a mirror still startles me. I groan at the damage I caused and can only hope for improvement in the future.

I have come a long way in finding myself since my suicide attempt, but I need to keep seeking.

When my time was ending at the mental health facility, I struggled with wanting to stay longer. A greater sense of confidence is only one of the benefits I had been gaining. I didn't want the growth to end.

During my years of marriage, I had shut everyone out, leaning on Taylor far too much. The friends I made at the facility taught me to open up and let more of who I was come out, with my flaws unhidden. It didn't matter that no one else there struggled with BDD specifically. Each of them had his or her own unique problems, but on some level we shared a camaraderie that reinforced my understanding that I didn't have to battle this illness alone.

My counselor and I talked long about what

life would be like on the outside. I worried about reverting to old patterns and wondered if living with my parents would help or hinder. The questions I had about going back into my old life kept pouring out of me and I tried to keep a sense of unease at bay.

I had begun my community service hours doing extra chores around the facility, but had no idea where I could complete them *out there.* I was anxious about how people would treat me on the streets, the coffee shops, the post office. The scars on my face were still thick and ropy, very visible to anyone who even glanced at me.

It had taken me months of baby steps to go out in public, and at first I needed someone with me at all times to even consider venturing beyond the walls of the mental health facility. My mom or a friend would pick me up and take me to the mall or out for coffee. The buffer they provided eased me into dealing with feeling self-conscious wherever I went.

Sometimes, however, their protection wasn't enough to shield me from reality. Taking the bus with a friend one day, a guy caught sight of me, pointed and shouted *"Hey! You are that girl from the news. You are more famous than I am!"* While every eye turned toward me, my friend and I sat there kind of shocked at his laughing manner. In hindsight I wish I had had the courage to answer him casually and deflate the tension everyone was feeling. Instead, I coped by trying to ignore him, quietly talking to my friend and looking out the window.

Maybe I will get better at this.
Maybe.
I hope.

That incident ranks tame in comparison to another. My friend, Dave and I were waiting at a bus stop as a car drove by with two female passengers. One of the gals whipped out her phone and took a picture of me while passing by. Seconds later we saw the same vehicle turn around and come back for another go, this time with a video camera. The window rolled down, camera rolling and the gal said, *"I can't believe it's you!"* Dave stepped in front of me and blocked their view, but the audacity had already done its damage.

Like a traveling show, I felt like I had become the new entertainment in town.

I found there is a definite downside to the ability to lip-read in situations like these. Growing up I learned to read people, catch nuances others wouldn't see and understand body language. While some trying-to-be-subtle gawkers think they are being discreet about their conversations, in my hyper-vigilance I know exactly what is being said. Dealing with the physical wounds is hard enough, but adding more emotional ones to my long history can make me feel like I am regressing in my attempts to get my life back rather than moving forward.

But I also am beginning to understand that strangers don't know my story and I shouldn't expect them to. I have to be at peace with myself at a deep level in order to not take the negative reactions personally. This is one more area in which I need to grow and reach for compassion and grace.

God loves me.
And He calls me to love others.

A few days after I left the mental health facility for good, I checked into the hospital for my first surgery. The plan was to shave my head and use the skin on my scalp to graft my left cheek and chin where the damage was most extensive. It turned out to be a longer process. My plastic surgeon used a medical product called Integra to prepare the area. It is a fake skin that helps to rebuild the underlying layer of damaged tissue. The actual grafting took place two weeks later.

The first round of grafting didn't turn out like we had hoped. My skin has a tendency toward keloid scars, the worst kind that grow beyond the actual wound site. None of us expected the scar lines to get so big and so out of control. Every person's skin reacts differently to damage. Unfortunately, mine is not the kind that heals well.

The second round of grafting attempted to redo the first. My choices were to use my scalp again or to have skin taken from my stomach as the donor site, followed by daily treatments in a hyperbaric chamber to promote healing.

The plan that got nixed was to put expanders under my skin to stretch it out over a four-month period. It would have involved adding liquid every week or two, as much as the skin could take at one time. Maybe this version will show up again in the future depending on the results from the current surgery. For the scars on my nose and right cheek, plan A was to cut them out and stitch them up but the results weren't positive. I'm not sure what Plan B will be.

Often I feel like I am in the middle of a sci-fi movie.

The emotional ups and downs, the waiting and wondering tax me in ways I never could have foreseen. It feels like a big medical experiment.

And it is.

All I can do is hold on to hope that my surgeon will do the best job possible. I have placed a lot of trust in his hands and am immensely thankful that he is committed to seeing this through.

I know I won't look like I used to, but what the final outcome will be is yet unknown. Reminding myself that I did this only makes it more unreal. Who was that girl who put acid on her face? I feel like I am that person no longer.

Grief.

Some days it pours out of me in waves. Other days I just hold it in and try to keep breathing. I go back and forth between despair and hope. And I pray that hope will win in the end. I pray for a miracle. But with help, I will deal with the outcome no matter what it is.

I have been told that in my younger years, joy would bubble out of me at times and spread to others. I want to recapture that. Real joy bursting through.

Bethany Joy.
I am alive.
I matter.

My amazing family and friends matter.
My hopes, dreams and fears matter. I am not alone. I love the possibility that there could be a purpose for the pain I have gone through, that maybe someone else out there could relate to me. Learn from my stubborn mistakes.

Maybe even find a grain of hope for his or her

life in my story.

I don't want anyone to go through what I did and my prayer is that they will be spared a similar fate. I am trusting God that He can use my pain to bring good into another's life.

I know what it is like to be lost on life's journey and to feel the disarray, the brokenness and helplessness. Being on the proper medication and dealing with my issues by getting professional help has brought me clarity like never before. I feel like I am more me than I have ever been. Even with the long road ahead of me, and a rough one behind.

Life looks different now.

I look different, but the lies are behind me.
I have faced the truth.
And trust it will keep setting me free.

"Then you will know the truth and the truth will set you free." John 8:32

A Note from Joe and Nancy

Do you know the saying, *hindsight is twenty-twenty?* It is so very true.

When they hand you your precious little one all wrapped up in a baby blanket at the hospital, you never imagine what life's struggles lie ahead for that child. You are so filled with bliss, joy and love, that your thoughts and hopes are always for a wonderful, better-than-we-had-it life. When a pregnant mom is asked about the gender of her baby, "Do you want a girl or a boy?", the answer is always, "We don't care as long as the baby is healthy."

Well, what if they aren't healthy? When we had our dear daughter, Bethany, we had no idea of her future, only that we loved her unconditionally just as our Father in heaven loves us. At the time, everything seemed perfect.

You may have asked yourself regarding Bethany's story, "why didn't her parents see this and do something about it sooner?" As many of you have experienced living with difficult family dynamics, such as alcoholism, abuse, anorexia or many other trials that people face, you tend to learn coping behaviors that become the norm.

What does that mean? Basically you learn to live with these illnesses and they become part of your every day life. You make excuses and justifications such as, "Oh, she's just crabby today" or "Teenagers always spend a lot of time in the bathroom." When we found Bethany's behavior excessive, we would address it and ask questions, but it always ended up with a family fight of some sort and we would chalk it up as "typical teenage girl behavior." She was very good at hiding her true illness, and promises of doing better just kept the cycle going on and on. As with anything not really dealt with, for a while it became all good again, and then it would slowly grow and we would confront it: "You are spending way too much time in the bathroom," or "Did you pick your skin again?" (thinking that she was obsessed with blemishes and not realizing there was way more to this). Then things would calm down, and slowly begin all over again.

So what did we do? Basically nothing. We didn't know she was sick. We just coped and thought she would grow out of it, not realizing the depth and disparity that she lived with every moment of her young life.

There's another reason we didn't ask any questions. The cross section of the community we were a part of was just not comfortable or even educated in the area of mental illness. There was a stigma that we wanted to avoid and so we tried to give the appearance that everything was perfect. How could it be perfect? We are not perfect! There is no blame on our community, in our work, church or school setting, but the lack of education in this area of the greater population did have an impact on our willingness to share. As we have come out on the other side we have realized how important it is to be educated in the area of mental illness, so that fear and stereotypes can be dispelled and healing can begin.

It breaks our hearts to know that Bethany went through all that virtually alone. We ask ourselves, "Why didn't we see it?" We just didn't. We are imperfect people loved by a perfect God. He forgives, He brings hope and faith, and joy comes in the morning. We now see.

Bethany is doing so very well, and we are very proud of her (and her siblings and family as well, of course). We love her so much and she brings us much joy and happiness. Also, our current church has shown us nothing but love and compassion, and some even have an understanding of mental illness and have helped us in our navigation of this life-long road. We are so thankful for the help that we have received from our family, friends, and church. We are also thankful to the supportive and understanding people in our community. We are finding there are many out there.

We understand the heartaches and the joys that parents face as their children grow. There are so many highs and lows. It was an extremely difficult road that we walked. You probably can't even imagine what we had to go through, but I am sure if any of you have children, you understand in some capacity, that you would do anything for them, and stand by them and love them no matter what.

Our hope is that what we experienced can now help you, that you can possibly avoid some of the pitfalls that we experienced as parents, so that you don't have to walk as far down that road as we had to. Some tools for you if you or a family member suffers from mental illness:

Ask questions. Seek professional help and ask, "Is this normal behavior for my son, or daughter?" We have found that the mental health care providers are amazing, truly care and have many tools for guidance and help available. Most of the help is free. If you don't "click" with one, or don't get answers, then try someone else. Don't give up.

God is good all the time. His love endures

forever. He is our peace, hope and joy.

He will show you the way. He showed us.

Resources

Books

The BDD Workbook: Overcome Body Dysmorphic Disorder and End Body Image Obsession by James Claiborn, Ph.D. and Cherry Pedrick, R.N. (New Harbinger Publications, 2002)

The Broken Mirror: Understanding and Treating Body Dysmorphic Disorder by Katharine Phillips (Oxford University Press, 2005)

Feeling Good About the Way You Look: A Program for Overcoming Body Dysmorphic Disorder by Sabine Wilhelm, Ph.D. (Guilford Press, 2006)

Living with Body Dysmorphic Disorder by Lea Walker with Janet Lee (Amazon, 2010)

Understanding Body Dysmorphic Disorder by Katharine Phillips (Oxford University Press, 2009)

Websites

http://www.adaa.org

http://www.bddcentral.com

https://www.mghocd.org

http://en.wikipedia.org

Acknowledgements

I am so thankful to everyone who has stood by me through everything.

First, I want to thank my Lord and Savior, Jesus. He is my Strength and Rock on which I stand. I shall forever seek His will. He shows me the way, the truth and the life.

Mom and Dad with your unending support and love - thank you for walking me through some of the worst days and always being by my side. I love you both more than you know.

Mom - for always being a rock - without you we would have all fallen apart. Thanks for giving me laughter, hugs - the cheesy commercials we do, the M&Ms, Skittles and TV shows - for reassuring me that life will be good again. You and Willow and I - Best Friends Forever. Love you "DM"!! "YT-Wink"

Dad - thanks for always checking in to make

sure I'm ok - for loving me, encouraging me and telling me I'm beautiful. I love your predictability - and giving me the first "hi" after work (sorry Momma). Thank you for making me laugh with your nerdy words. Love you, "Daaaad."

My sister, Willow, aka Rene, who knows and gets me more than anyone - over and over you have given me the gift of inspiration and hope, painting a bright future beyond these scars, and a word from God that He has me in the palm of His hand. I am so blessed to have you in my life. Yes, I will buy coffee. "YT"

Scott - thank you for not being judgmental. You are the best brother-in-law I could ask for. I admire you for being such a great husband and dad. I love our conversations about food. "Hot or cold?"

Abro - thanks for always making me laugh, for seeing my sadness and caring to lift my spirits. Your support and protection even amidst the clowning around will always stay with me. Thanks for loving me and telling me I am beautiful and that I matter. "Maroon." Love you, Morcron!!

Boone, a new and best friend - thanks for urging me on and helping me to not give up when those feelings of despair hit hard. You were always there for me. I count on your advice, support and laughter. And yes, someday you will get your $99 even though I won. "Wink"

David - I am glad we found each other at the facility to get through the rough points. You brought fun when there was so little to laugh about. We will always have "metal detecting."

Stan and Kathy, our pastors and friends for so many years - thank you for your love and support. You were there from the early years on. Thanks for believing in me and loving me no matter what.

Christine "C. Stick" - I think you are the best. And so dear to my heart. Thank you for keeping in touch. Love you!

Pastor Scott, Pastor Jeremy, Lynette, Julia, Darcie, Russ, Sandi, aka Savvys, Treese and Misty- you were there for me through thick and thin with your visits, cards, texts and letters. Thanks for all of the hope they gave, for your prayers, concern and support.

My counselors from the mental health facility - thank you for helping me when I was in such dire need. You gave me strength and hope that all would be ok. Your guidance led me to cope. To Kathy especially, I appreciate all of your help.

My lawyers, Andrew Wheeler and Chad Sleight, who worked tirelessly on my case - I will never forget how you went beyond the job to support me emotionally, being by my side every step of the way. I appreciate you both.

The Oregon Burn Center and all of the staff - I want to convey a HUGE thank you for all of your care and support.
To Doctor Eshraghi - thanks for taking care of me despite the circumstances and following up on my injuries.
And to Doctor Vangelisti - for taking over, showing genuine care and keeping hope alive. Thank you for being invested in the process and sticking with me to the end.

Ashley - thank you for your insights and for staying in touch. I have never laughed with anyone the way I can with you. I think you are an amazing wife, mom, daughter and friend. "Your love is a one in a million." Love you, Ash.

Naphy - I adore you for being so real and loyal, for not judging me, for being a long-term friend that wants the best for my future. Always remember, "Hunts." I love you.

Joe "Bear"- thank you for bringing me laughter and helping me forget about my struggles. You have become a best friend and I love you dearly. "Where are we?!?"

Mona - you have become someone I call a real close friend, someone I trust and love dearly. Thank you for all of your love, support and hard work. For everything you have done. For not giving up on me. One day all the

Starbucks coffee will be on me! "Wink"

Love,
Bethany

Write me at:

facingthetruth2013@gmail.com

About the Author

With Master degrees in both
Pastoral Studies and Social Work,
Mona draws on her experience
of being burned as a teenager
to reach out to trauma survivors.
After living and working in Southern Russia
as an ESL teacher
and humanitarian aid advocate
for over a decade,
she is now living stateside and recently
published her own survival story:
Sage Was The Perfect Shadow,
available on Amazon.

To visit her blog,
go to monakrueger.com

Cover Design by JaneInk.com

Cover Photo by Rayhendricksphotography.com

Made in the USA
Lexington, KY
25 March 2013